Black and White with Shades of Grey

Black and White with Shades of Grey

An Introduction to the Strategy of Test Cricket

by

Tony Whelpton

TD PUBLICATIONS

TD Publications, 271 Gloucester road, Cheltenham, GL51 7AA
Telephone 01242 236692, Fax 01242 236693
E-mail cricket@tdpublications.co.uk
Website: http://www.tdpublications.co.uk

Printed by Bell & Bain Ltd, Glasgow

To the memory of my father, Frank Whelpton,
who once bowled me an over so bad
that the bowler at the other end got me out
because I couldn't bat for laughing
– proving to me that cricket is basically a psychological game,
which is the theme of this book

Introduction

To the uninitiated, a game of cricket appears to be simply a matter of one person throwing a ball for another to hit and someone else to fetch, whereupon it starts all over again. But if that were all it involved, is it really likely that so many people would be willing to spend six hours a day, for five days at a time, doing it? Would the game have continued to fascinate some of the world's great intellects over such a long period of time? And would this fascination have spread its net to countries as far apart, both physically and culturally, as India, Pakistan, Australia and the West Indies? Clearly there must be more to it than that.

In fact, as I implied in my earlier book *How's That! A Layman's Guide to Cricket* when I said cricket was a bit like chess, it is the thinking that is going on behind the action that provides the more enduring interest: cricket, at its highest level, is no more and no less than psychological warfare, and it is my intention in this book to examine some of the thought-processes which lie behind the action.

It would have been possible to write such a book in purely theoretical terms, with just a few concrete examples here and there to help it along, but that wouldn't have made a very interesting book, nor would it have made much contribution towards enhancing the reader's enjoyment and appreciation of a live game. Instead, I decided to base everything on what took place in a number of actual matches and, since the matches in which the best thinkers and practitioners of the game operate are grouped in series, with the thinking in one game affected by the situation in the series as a whole, I decided to use the most recent test series between England and the West Indies, all the matches taking place in England during the summer of 2000.

I have deliberately chosen to concentrate on test cricket rather than the one-day version of the game, not because I feel that the one-day game is inferior but because it is quite different. It is perhaps inferior in that there is insufficient time available for all the subtleties of five-day strategy, but it has a strategy of its own which could very well merit a book in its own right.

I hope that concentrating on a whole series of matches between two countries will help to reinforce the notion that cricket is a psychological battle, and that in many ways it is a battle between the two captains. Thus this book could also have been called Adams versus Hussain, for it is essentially the story of their personal battle; in the event, of course, such a title would not have been appropriate because Nasser Hussain was unable to play in the Second Test because of injury, and his place was taken by Alec Stewart.

The series turned out to be one of the most exciting I have experienced in over fifty years of watching test cricket, and working on a book such as this has been a great joy, a privilege even. I do not profess to know all the answers as far as cricket strategy is concerned – who does! – But I hope that those readers who know as much if not more about the strategy of the game as I do will none the less derive great pleasure from re-living this series viewing it from this particular angle.

I must stress that this is an *introduction* to the strategy of cricket, and the analysis which I have provided only just scratches the surface. It could not be otherwise without becoming tedious, because in reality the captain is considering different options after each ball is bowled, and it would obviously be impossible, not to say undesirable, to provide that sort of detail in a book such as this.

I am much indebted to various people for their invaluable help, including Paul McGregor, a photographer whose work you are likely to see whenever you pick up a newspaper, and who kindly supplied the photographs at the head of the chapters on the Headingley and the Oval tests (to which he retains the copyright), Clare Fathers of the England and Wales Cricket Board, Stuart Weatherhead of the MCC, and to countless others who have offered me help and advice.

One final word: this book assumes the reader already has a certain amount of knowledge as to how the game works. If you don't yet understand the basics, then you need to look first at my other book, *How's That! A Layman's Guide to Cricket* (TD Publications, 1998), and then come back to this one. Then, I hope, you'll start to derive as much enjoyment as I do from watching the game.

Tony Whelpton
Cheltenham, November 2000

How it works in theory

The Captain is God!

The ultimate strategy in a game of cricket depends on the captain of each team; he at least formulates the game-plan and orchestrates the tactics employed during most of the game.

But, although the captain will often get the blame when his side loses, especially if a whole series has been lost, it's not always his fault, because he can't really control the efficiency of his players. One of the mysteries of the universe, at least as far as Christians are concerned, is the existence of an omnipotent deity who has endowed his servants with the gift of exercising free will only to see them frequently straying from the strait and narrow; the cricket captain, like God, is responsible for the overall strategy, but his players may be unable or unwilling to put it into practice!

The strategy employed will always tend to reflect the personality of the captain. Some team captains are fairly conservative by nature, whilst others tend to be a bit more adventurous. Which of the three captains involved in this series is which (there were three because Stewart took over while Hussain was injured) will become clearer as the book progresses.

| Nasser Hussain | Jimmy Adams | Alec Stewart |

Team selection

The selection of the team may not be altogether the responsibility of the captain. As far as an international team is concerned, the team willnormally be picked by a selection committee, of whom the captain invariably forms part, and he would expect to have a considerable amount of say over who goes in and who is left out.

Of course any selection depends on the players available; there is, for instance, no point in deciding that you'd like to include a left-arm wrist-spinner if there's no such bowler available to play. That said, there are a number of matters to be taken into consideration: the current form of the players in question, the nature of the pitch on which the game will be played, the strengths and weaknesses of the opposition, the balance of the side, etc., etc.

The first decision will probably be how many bowlers to include. This isn't always a straightforward matter, for the answer may very well depend on how good your best bowlers are at batting. If you decide to include five specialist bowlers none of whom is capable of scoring more than a handful of runs, then you're putting considerable pressure on the remaining six players to score highly. And if your wicketkeeper is not too good a batsman either, then the dilemma becomes even worse. But generally speaking, the better the pitch for batting, the more bowlers you are likely to need.

Occasionally a side may have an all-rounder who is equally good with bat or with ball, which obviously makes the matter of selection that much easier. But truly great all-rounders are rare: the fact that most people are able to come up with names like Keith Miller, Kapil Dev and Ian Botham, and that England have been searching for a 'new Botham' ever since the old one retired, only serves to underline just how rare a breed they are.

The selection committee will have a pretty good idea of what sort of bowling tends to do well on a particular ground. On some grounds, spinners never prosper; on others they have a consistently good record. Consequently one of the first decisions to be made will be whether to include a spin-bowler or not – or even two, because, especially in India and Pakistan, a pitch may be tailor-made to take spin and be quite unresponsive to fast bowling (which explains why India and Pakistan have produced so many great spin bowlers over the years, and why India are almost unbeatable in India but have a pretty dismal record elsewhere in the world). If a spinner is included, you then have to decide how many seamers to put in the team: three may well be enough if the wicket really is taking spin, but if one of them should pull a muscle and be unable to bowl, or be temporarily out of form, you could be in trouble.

Then there is the matter of batting-order. If your wicketkeeper is also a very good opening batsman, as is the case with England's Alec Stewart, you have to decide whether it's fair to ask him to do both jobs; if, for instance, the other side batted for the first day and a half and he'd been keeping wicket for all that time, with all the concentration that implies, is it reasonable to expect him to go straight out and spend the rest of the day batting, as you'd normally hope your openers would? If England were to bat first there'd be less of a problem, and some commentators have suggested that Stewart's position could vary according to the circumstances, but it's not quite as straightforward as that: to begin with, statistics suggest that Stewart scores more runs when he opens the innings. Moreover, quite a lot of other players feel that they can only score runs when they bat in a particular position – they may be right, they may be wrong, but it's something that can easily become a self-fulfilling prophecy.

Again, as far as the opening pair are concerned, there's a lot to be said for choosing one who tends to be positive and free-scoring, and one who is perhaps slower to score runs but who is very obdurate and difficult to remove; such a player can be invaluable in holding a side together when things are going against them. (Michael Atherton is a case in point – there have been many occasions when he has proved an effective anchor, and quite a few when his early dismissal has apparently led the rest of the team to collective suicide.)

A balance of left-hand and right-hand opening batsmen is also a good thing to have. In the series under review England had Atherton or Ramprakash (right-hand) and Knight or Trescothick (left-hand), whilst the West Indies had Gayle or Griffith (left-hand) and Campbell (right-hand). There are at least two advantages in this: first of all the alternation of right and left-hand batsmen can disturb the rhythm of a bowler and make it difficult for him, and secondly the constant necessity to change the field according to whether the batsman is left- or right-handed can become irritating and/or tiring for the fielding side.

Pitch and Toss

The title I've chosen for this section might perhaps suggest a gambling game, and it certainly happens on occasions that winning or losing the toss has an undue effect on the final outcome of the game. For this reason, some observers have proposed various other ways of deciding who should bat first, but as yet there is a long way to go before consensus is achieved on this issue.

One of the first things the captain has to do is to have a good look at the weather (and the weather-forecast), inspect the pitch, and decide what he will do if he wins the toss. (If he loses the toss, there's nothing he can do about it – he has to go along with what the opposing captain decides, although, as we shall see in the case of some of the matches in this series, the outcome of the toss would have been the same whichever captain had been given the choice.) The tradition in test cricket is to bat first if you win the toss, but sometimes, as we shall see, conditions can be so favourable to the bowlers at the beginning of a match that it would be silly not to give your bowlers the opportunity to exploit them and establish an immediate advantage.

But it will not necessarily always be the way the pitch is likely to play in the first few hours that determines the decision. There may be indications that, once the first session is safely negotiated, the pitch will become a very good pitch to bat on, and it may very well be a good idea to have first use of it and put a good score on the board, thus creating pressure in a different way. And if it looks as if the pitch is likely to wear badly over the course of five days' play, and therefore be very responsive to spin-bowling on the last day, you might like to consider whether you would prefer the other side's spinner or yours to benefit from those conditions. But reading a pitch is a very inexact science, and all captains sometimes make choices that they later come to regret.

Batting strategy

Except when he's batting himself, there's little the batting side's captain can do to influence what's happening in the middle. He can, of course, issue instructions at the start of an innings as to the basic approach to be used. He might say, for instance, 'For the first hour, just concentrate on staying in. It doesn't matter about runs, they'll come once you get settled. Just make sure you don't get out.' On the other hand, he might say, 'We need a positive start. One of you should concentrate on staying in at all costs, but the other should take every opportunity to score runs. Don't take too many risks, but if you take the first run quickly you'll often find that you can run two instead of just one. Try and put the bowlers and the fielders under pressure'.

In between overs you'll sometimes see the batting side's twelfth man come on to the field carrying a pair of batting gloves. The natural assumption is that the batsman needs a change of gloves because his hands are sweaty, but if you look carefully you'll often see the same pair of gloves being carried back to the pavilion. What has really happened is that the twelfth man has brought fresh instructions from the captain, and the batting gloves were just a pretext.

Apart from the two approaches mentioned above, there are a number of other tactics which may be employed by batsmen, for instance:

Rotating the strike

The batsmen take as many singles as possible so they are regularly changing ends. This is particularly effective if a left-hander and a right-hander are batting together, because it means the bowler has to change his line of delivery and thus can't settle into a constant rhythm, and the fielders have to change positions each time the batsmen change ends.

Farming the bowling

Sometimes the batsmen will try to avoid running singles, in order to stay at the same end. This can happen, for instance, if one of them finds a particular bowler difficult to deal with, and the batsmen agree between them to take one bowler each. (Needless to say, the fielding side will usually be aware of this, and will do their best to frustrate them.) It can also happen, especially towards the end of an innings, if one batsman is well established and the other one is a not very competent tail-ender. In this case the good batsman will probably try to score boundaries or twos early in the over, and take a single or a three from the fifth or sixth ball, leaving the tail-ender only one or two balls to face. Here again, the fielding side will be only too aware of this tactic, and will do their best to stop it working.

Attack or defence?

The captain must constantly be re-assessing the position of the match and considering when it's appropriate to attack and when it's appropriate to defend. Generally speaking the bowling side will attack at the start of any batsman's innings or at the start of any session of play, or at any time they appear to have established an advantage. It goes almost without saying that in these situations the batting side will tend to go on the defensive, although particular circumstances may dictate otherwise; some lower-order batsmen, for instance, may not be very good at constantly playing a dead bat, but tend to be good strikers of the ball, and in this case they may decide that carrying the attack to the bowler is the best form of defence. Naturally, this approach does not always work!

For the batting side, an attacking strategy involves taking more risks. A batsman simply intent on keeping his wicket intact will avoid playing an aggressive stroke to all but the really bad balls, i.e. those that are wide of the stumps and short-pitched or even half-volleys; even then he'll try and play his aggressive strokes along the ground. The batsman in really attacking mode will play an aggressive shot to all but the best deliveries, and will hit the ball in the air too – with the intention, of course, of either clearing the boundary or getting the ball past close-in fielders.

As for the fielding side, their attacking strategy is a matter of thoughtful bowling and careful field-placing, and both of these topics are covered elsewhere.

Motivation

In theory there should be no problem motivating a team at the beginning of a match, but there will inevitably be moments when something occurs which causes an individual's head to go down – or even the heads of the entire team. A long spell without taking a wicket, a decision which went the wrong way, a misfield, a dropped catch (especially depressing for the bowler) – all of these can have a demoralising effect, and it's up to the captain to make sure that everyone keeps their eye on the matter in hand. After all, even if the batsman is

150 not out, there's nothing to say he won't be out next ball, and if he is, then another wicket could easily go down too, and the situation would be very different.

It is made quite clear by former England captain Mike Brearley in his excellent book *The Art of Captaincy* that the captain needs to be something of a psychologist, citing as examples the different approaches he needed to use in order to get the best out of players like Bob Willis and Ian Botham. Whether to make a bowling change may just as easily be a question of individual psychology as of assessing the match situation.

A team is made up of individuals, some of whom will respond to encouragement but not to criticism, whilst others will respond to harsh words by bowling with more aggression; it is the captain's job, in short, to know how to get the best out of each individual.

This implies a lot of work on the part of the captain before the match even starts; he needs to know his team's strengths and weaknesses not only in cricketing terms but also in terms of personality. But he also needs to study the opposition in the same way, finding out, for instance, how different individuals react to pressure, how they are normally dismissed or how they score most of their runs when batting, or how they normally get their wickets when bowling.

Above all the captain must lead by example, especially where body-language is concerned. However depressed or worried he may be about the current match-situation, he must guard against letting it show – not just to avoid boosting the morale of the opposition, but to prevent loss of concentration in his own side, because lack of concentration leads to mistakes, and mistakes lead to lost matches.

Line and length

This is something you'll hear commentators talking about a great deal, especially if the bowlers are not having much success and the commentators are trying to explain why. In theory the perfect length is one which has the batsman in two minds as to whether to play forward or back, whilst the ideal line is two or three inches outside the off stump – the so-called 'corridor of uncertainty', where the batsman has difficulty deciding whether it's safe to leave the ball alone.

Of course, if all bowlers stuck rigidly to this strategy few batsmen would ever be out bowled or caught at fine leg. It would also allow the batsman to settle into a groove and play more comfortably, which is the opposite of what the bowler wants to achieve. Consequently variety of line and length is also important: something unexpected will often catch a batsman unawares and lead him into a false shot.

But there are times when nothing seems to work, and then an ability to revert to the classic good line and length with just the occasional variation will at least make the batsman think, and coupled with judicious field-placing, restrict run-scoring opportunities in such a way that the batsman starts to take risks out of frustration. Sometimes the nature of the pitch, coupled with the weather conditions, is such that it seems the bowlers only have to find the right line and length in order to take wickets – there are one or two occasions such as this in the matches we shall discuss later. In theory all first-class bowlers are capable of finding that line and length, but in practice all sorts of factors – psychological or physical – may make it difficult for a particular bowler to do it on a particular day. Moreover inaccuracy can be catching: if one bowler constantly goes astray, the others can easily catch the disease.

Variation of line

As far as line is concerned, a bowler may decide to bowl either at the wicket or to one side or the other. But when we say that, we're talking about the ultimate destination of the ball, and further variety can be introduced by changing the angle of delivery. Thus a bowler may decide to bowl 'over' the wicket (where the hand in which he holds the ball is the one nearer the stumps at the bowler's end) or 'round' the wicket (where the ball is in the hand further away from the stumps).

And then the bowler can change the angle even more by bowling either very close to the stumps or from the extreme edge of the return crease. But there may be a price to pay for varying the angle: a right-arm bowler who bowls round the wicket to a right-handed batsman will find it difficult to win lbw decisions, especially if he is bowling from wide of the crease, because the angle of flight is such that even a ball pitched on the stumps would have to turn back to leg a great deal if it were to hit the wicket, and it would be difficult for the umpire to be absolutely certain, as he must be, that it would turn enough.

The bowler might consider that a price worth paying, however. If, for instance, the batsman seems determined to hit everything towards the leg boundary, bowling round the wicket and directing the ball towards slip might be a way of inducing a false stroke. If the batsman is particularly strong on the off side, bowling over the wicket and angling the ball towards his legs might be the more effective strategy.

Or it might not. After all, the batsman isn't going to allow himself to be dictated to if he can possibly avoid it, and he may very well vary his stance or shot-selection accordingly, thus neutralising the bowler's strategy.

In other words, here, as in every other area of the game, the only really good strategy is the one that works. When you've persevered with one tactic for a while without achieving any success, you need to try something else. And when you're completely out of ideas, then you revert to line and length, because that's where the percentages are more in your favour.

Night-watchmen

Any batsman is most vulnerable at the start of his innings, even the best. Consequently, if a wicket falls shortly before the close of play, a captain might decide to protect the batsman who would normally go in next by sending in a 'night-watchman', someone who normally bats lower in the order. The theory is that he will probably not make many runs wherever he bats, and if he gets out quickly it's a shame but not necessarily a catastrophe. And if, as sometimes happens, he manages not only to stay in until the close of play but manages to score quite a few runs the following morning, that's an added bonus. Needless to say, it doesn't always work, and the opponents of such a strategy would say that if you want to avoid a wicket falling, it is the good batsman rather than the more moderate one who is more likely to succeed. As always, there are no hard and fast rules!

Statistics

The uninitiated might think that the preoccupation with statistics which seems to affect many cricket enthusiasts is simply an esoteric by-product of the game, but in reality it can serve a genuine purpose. It has already been suggested that the captain needs to be aware of the strengths and weaknesses not only of his own side but also of the opposition, and a study of the statistics of the game is one useful way of achieving this. One also speaks a great deal of 'playing the percentages'; it is only by the keeping of statistics that anyone knows what the percentages are, so all players ignore them at their peril.

Pressure and intimidation

Cricket is a psychological game, and the side that wins is the one which is better able to handle pressure. But there are many ways of exerting pressure. A compulsive hooker is put under pressure by bowling short and placing men in positions where his hook shot may be caught. One who likes to score quickly may be put under pressure by restricting his scoring opportunities. A bowler is put under pressure by negating his tactics, whether by a change of stance, moving down the pitch to smother his spin, taking quick singles, judicious use of the pads, or even on occasion by playing unorthodox shots. A fielder is put under pressure by running the first run quickly so that he has half an eye on the batsmen and only half an eye on the ball. And so on – the possibilities are endless.

But pressure can turn into intimidation, and cricket history is littered with occasions when relations between teams – or even nations – have been soured by intimidatory tactics; this has often been a matter of bowling fast at the body – or even the head. In recent years improvements in the effectiveness of various forms of body-armour has led to a reduction in the degree of physical danger, and the bowling of fast, short-pitched deliveries is considered a legitimate means of applying pressure as long as it is not overdone.

Intimidation may, of course, assume a psychological rather than a physical form, and this is one area of the modern first-class game which the authorities are even now trying their best to control. Some individuals – and some teams – make a habit of saying things (whether to their face or which they are intended to overhear) which are intended to disturb an opponent's concentration. Needless to say, such things vary from the relatively innocuous to the downright unpleasant, obscene, or even racist.

Most fair-minded commentators and players would take the view that pressure, and even intimidation, are part of the game as long as the means used are cricketing means. To indulge in 'sledging', as it is termed, which involves comments about the opponent's personal life which have nothing to do with cricket, should be as foreign to the game as throwing the ball at an opponent's head. And that's all one should need to say about it.

The new ball

In first-class matches the bowling side is allowed to take a new ball after eighty overs have been bowled with the old one, and in most cases it is taken at the earliest possible opportunity because the new ball – the bright red cherry, as some commentators refer to it – tends to swing and bounce more, and being in possession of a bright new ball can bring renewed zest to a fast bowler, or even to the entire fielding side.

There are occasions, however, when a side may delay taking the new ball. It may be that a particular bowler is having great success with the old ball; maybe a fast bowler is producing reverse swing, or a slow bowler is getting it to spin viciously. It may be that, towards the end of the day conditions are somewhat damp, and the captain decides to wait until the next day rather than risk getting the new ball wet and having it lose its shine too quickly. It may also be that the softness of the old ball is making it difficult for the batsmen to score runs, and the hardness of the new ball would make run-scoring easier. Or it might even be that the bowlers who would normally take the new ball are simply too tired to bowl any more, as might happen towards the end of a long day in the field in a hot climate, although one would hope the captain would have worked out his bowling changes in such a way as to prevent that happening.

Short-term v long-term

There are occasions, especially in test cricket, when the strategy is determined, or at least affected, by circumstances external to the actual game being played. The most obvious of these would be where a side is one match down in a five-match series, with only three matches left to play; to lose the third would make it impossible to win the series, and so it becomes imperative not to take unnecessary risks over declarations or chasing a virtually impossible target. Such risks are more often seen either when a series is already won or lost, or when a side is trying to win the final test, which would enable them to level the series.

It can also happen that, although normally the immediate objective of a fielding side is to get a batsman out, the circumstances of the game suggest that they might actually be better off not taking a wicket: if the batting side need quick runs and both batsmen are struggling to score more than the odd single, the knowledge that the next man in is a notoriously successful big-hitter can make the bowlers uncommonly reluctant to take wickets!

Follow-on

If the side batting second are more than 200 runs behind on first innings in a five-day match, or more than 150 behind in a three- or four-day match, they may be asked to bat again. Whether they do so or not is entirely up to the opposing captain, who may however decide that it is in his team's interest to bat again rather than enforce the follow-on. Such circumstances might be if the lead was only just over 200 (or 150) and he thought the pitch was likely to deteriorate to such an extent that batting last would be

next to impossible. He might also decide not to enforce it if his side had spent a long time in the field and his bowlers were tired, or one of his key bowlers was carrying an injury.

Bowling changes

This can be one of the most difficult areas of the game for a captain, and games are won and lost by bowling changes being made (or not) at the right time. The good captain handles his bowlers astutely; he knows their capabilities, and doesn't make them bowl too long a spell, he knows whether they bowl better into or with the wind, or, where there is a slope (as at Lord's), from which end they are likely to be more effective.

He is also a good reader of the game, and knows when it is time for a change; the batsmen are showing signs of getting used to a particular kind of bowling, or a new batsman has come in and he knows that he is vulnerable to, say, a left-arm spinner early in his innings, etc. He must also keep an eye on how many overs are left before the new ball may be taken, so that he can make sure his new-ball bowlers are not too tired to use it when it comes.

One of his most difficult decisions can be if he is himself a bowler; deciding whether or when to put himself on to bowl, and, sometimes more crucially, when to take himself off, is a matter which on occasions has been known to win or lose matches.

The orthodox practice is to start with the two most effective fast bowlers, changing one of them perhaps after five or six overs if he hasn't yet taken a wicket, whilst keeping the other going for a further two or three overs, so that some sort of 'staggering' is achieved. It is comparatively rare in the first-class game to find the bowlers being changed at both ends at once: to do so would tend to jeopardise the rhythm and continuity of the attack.

Declaration

This is another difficult decision for a captain, because declaring the innings closed almost invariably involves taking certain risks. The object of a declaration must always be to gain an advantage whilst taking the smallest possible risk, but it can also involve making an offer which is tempting enough to make the other side think they are in with a chance. As with other aspects of the game, this is an area discussed at length, and very usefully, in Mike Brearley's *The Art of Captaincy*.

In recent years it has sometimes happened that the two captains have actually discussed with each other the matter of declaration, with a view to getting a result in an otherwise pointless game. This is more likely to happen in a County match than a test match, but there was a remarkable example of it in the 1999-2000 England v South Africa series, when both captains forfeited an innings in a match which had been severely truncated by rain. This, however, was such an unusual occurrence that, when the South African captain Hansie Cronje admitted taking money from a bookmaker in the course of this series, this was the first match to be regarded with suspicion.

An enterprising captain can sometimes gain an advantage by making a surprise declaration. In the match between England and Zimbabwe played at Trent Bridge at the beginning of June 2000, Zimbabwe declared their first innings closed when still 99 runs short of the England total, then dismissed England in their second innings for 147; if the match had not been severely curtailed by rain, this courageous declaration might have won them the match. At the same time, however, it is unlikely that such a declaration would have been made if Zimbabwe had not already been one match down in a two-match series.

Field-placing

The art of field-placing is a complex one; a thorough knowledge of your bowlers and of the batsmen's strengths and weaknesses are essential, and an understanding of geometry is a great help too. What's more, setting a defensive field when you should be attacking (or vice versa) is something that can lose matches, or even series.

And yet in theory placing a field is a simple matter. You only have nine men to put in position (the other two being the wicket-keeper and the bowler), and they have to protect the whole field. But theory and practice are by no means the same thing! The first decision must be how to split them up: 4/5 (four on one side of the wicket, five on the other) or 6/3 – or, very occasionally, 7/2. (There was a famous occasion when Dennis Lillee bowled with nine slips against New Zealand at Auckland in 1977, but few bowlers could bowl to such a field and get away with it!)

The next decision is whether you want an attacking or a defensive field. An attacking field for a fast bowler would probably mean four slips and a gully; a defensive field would have two slips, a gully and a third man. You also need to consider what type of shots you want to encourage the batsman to play, but, bearing in mind that some positions, notably fine leg, mid-on and cover are

virtually indispensable, the basic field-setting almost dictates itself once the split and the attack/defence questions have been answered. After that the skill lies in the fine-tuning: how deep do they need to be? Do they need to be close enough to save a single, or should they be out protecting the boundary?

On the following pages you will find examples of typical field-settings for various types of bowler. In a real situation you will find a number of changes being made to these patterns, some subtle, some drastic; the exact placings will depend on the strengths and weaknesses of the batsmen, the condition of the pitch, the state of the match, etc. We shall look at individual field-placings in particular circumstances later in the book, in the hope that those will do something to clarify the general picture.

Fast-medium out-swing

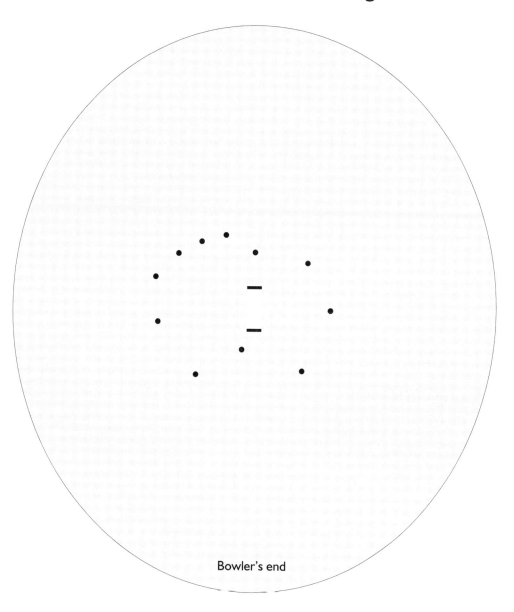

Bowler's end

This is an attacking field set to a right-handed batsman, assuming that the ball pitched on or just outside off-stump is swinging away from the batsman. If conditions are really favourable for the bowler and the batsman is in difficulties, he might change to a 7/2 split, moving a man from square-leg to third slip and moving mid-on to the mid-wicket position.

Fast-medium in-swing

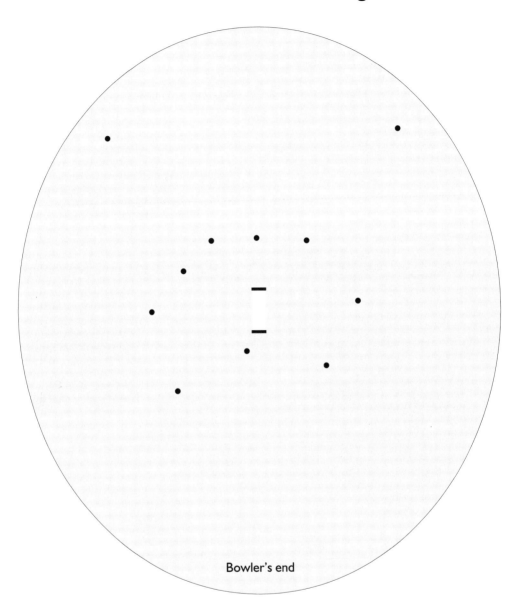

Bowler's end

This is a fairly orthodox field set for an in-swing bowler to a right-handed batsman, although you will often find one of the off-side fielders being moved in close on the leg-side if the ball is swinging to any marked degree.

Defensive medium-pace

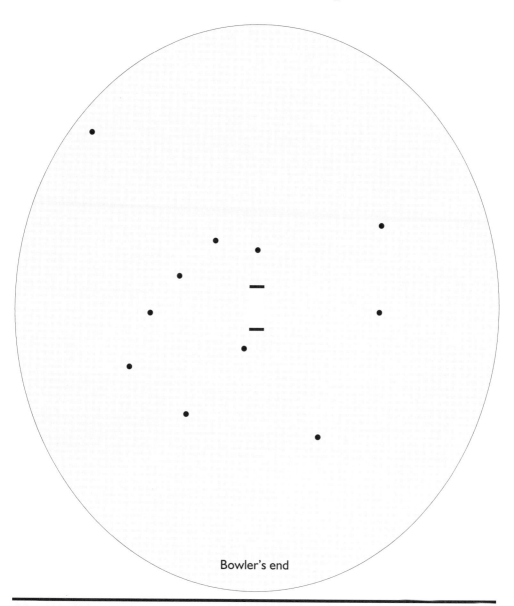

Bowler's end

This assumes that the bowler is bowling consistently just outside the line of off-stump (to a right-handed batsman). If the batsman tries to counter-attack by pulling the ball to leg, it might be necessary to move one of the off-side fielders to the leg-side, but it depends how successfully the batsman plays his shots: if he is not timing the ball well, it might be better to encourage him to persevere with that tactic for a while, in the hope that he will mistime a shot and be caught.

Off-spin

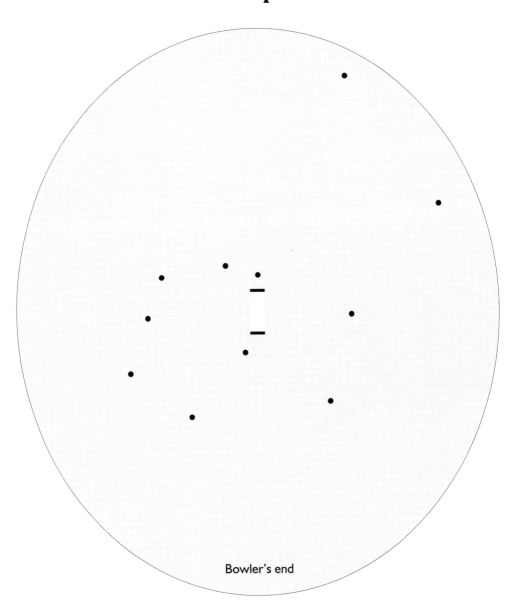

Bowler's end

This field-setting assumes that the pitch is not taking a lot of spin. On a pitch which is taking spin, fine-leg would probably come into a close catching position and deep extra-cover could move to forward short-leg for bat-pad catches. Again the assumption is made that the bowler is aiming on or just outside off-stump (to a right-handed batsman).

Leg-spin/googly

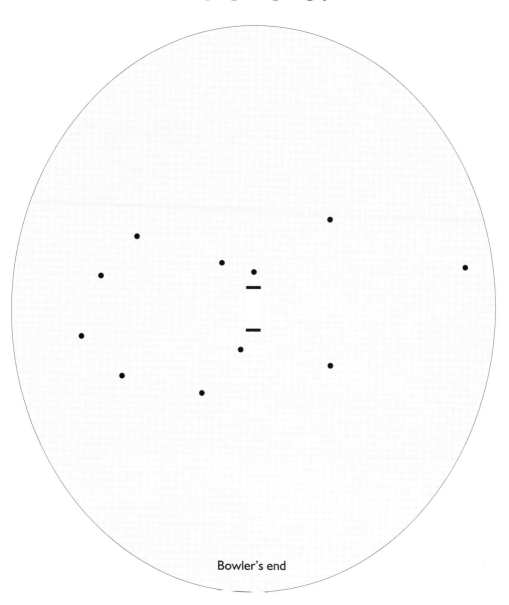

Bowler's end

This field-setting also assumes that the pitch is not taking a lot of spin. On a pitch which is taking spin, an extra slip would be put in place, fine-leg would move into a closer catching position and deep square-leg might move squarer. Again the assumption is made that the bowler is aiming on or just outside off-stump (to a right-handed batsman).

How it works in practice
England v West Indies 2000

Background to the series

Despite furrowed brows and gnawed-down finger-nails, English cricket supporters are incurably optimistic, always confident that a reverse in the fortunes of their national test team is just around the corner. Recent wins against Zimbabwe and in the final test of the South African tour did something to renew those hopes, whilst a feeling that the West Indies were considerably weaker than they had been for many years had encouraged the thought that this latest series would be much less one-sided than had generally been the case in recent years: not since 1969 had England won a series against the West Indies.

At the same time, even the most confirmed optimist recognised that it would be no push-over, especially when the news broke that Brian Lara, who had scored a world-record 375 against England in 1994, was returning from his self-imposed rest with a statement to the effect that he was keen to start scoring runs again – and a century against Zimbabwe at Arundel a few days before the Edgbaston test seemed to underline that keenness. In addition, the veteran fast bowler Courtney Walsh had just become the leading wicket-taker in test history (435 wickets), and he would still be partnered by Curtley Ambrose, whose own tally of 377 was more than that of any English bowler except Ian Botham (383). On the batting side, moreover, the presence of Jimmy Adams and Shivnarine Chanderpaul meant that they should not be under-estimated in that department either.

A thirst for victory on the part of the English was also undoubtedly fuelled by speculation that their victory in the final test against South Africa earlier in the year had been less than genuine; the South African captain at the time, Hansie Cronje, had denied actually 'throwing' matches, but many felt that this could well have been a match in which decisions had been taken for non-cricketing reasons. Indeed confirmation was received during the match that Cronje had taken money as an inducement to make a 'sporting' declaration in that match.

This meant that early confirmation was needed to the effect that an English revival really was on the way.

But the West Indians needed a victory just as much as the English. Having been accustomed to being regarded as one of the strongest sides in world cricket, they found their recent failures, especially against New Zealand, very hard to take, whilst the future of the game in the West Indies was also threatened by the tendency of youngsters to be more interested in basketball than cricket.

The game of cricket itself, however, was even more in need of an exciting series than were the two sides involved, such had been the fall-out from the South African match-fixing scandal. A general feeling that a match between England and the West Indies would be played strictly according to the letter and the spirit of the laws of cricket (and let us pray that such trust is not misplaced), coupled with the knowledge that any game of cricket involving the West Indies contains a large element of carnival, ensured that this series as much as any other was universally contemplated with eager anticipation.

The captains

Nasser Hussain is a batsman who, prior to this series, had played 49 times for England and had scored more than 3,000 runs at an average of just over 38 runs per innings, which is good, but not as high as one expects of a top-class batsman; moreover his recent batting form had been poor. Of the team assembled for this test, however, only Atherton and Stewart had a higher average than Hussain. He is still relatively inexperienced as a captain, but has the reputation of being a shrewd thinker both on and off the field, and appears to be well respected by his players.

Jimmy Adams has a better test record than Nasser Hussain, having scored his 2,500 runs at an average of just over 47, as well as having taken 22 wickets with his slow left-arm spinners. He is a quiet, undemonstrative man off the field, and his batting style is accumulative rather than flashy, but, although he has been captain of the West Indies for only a few months, he too is highly respected. By nature reluctant to take risks, he is nonetheless a pro-active captain, always on the move, always motivating his players.

The First Test

The Weather

So far the summer had been more than usually damp and cold; indeed on the day before the match torrential rain had flooded the ground, and only frantic work by the ground staff coupled with a dramatic improvement in the weather enabled the game to start on time. But the improvement was forecast to continue – in fact a heatwave was expected during the weekend.

The Pitch

Although the pitch itself had been covered throughout the whole of the previous day's rain, it was clearly very damp – perhaps because of 'sweating' beneath the tarpaulin, perhaps simply because that covering had delayed the normal drying-out process. At all events, it promised to be helpful to seam and swing in the early stages of the match, and since the West Indian attack was composed almost entirely of pace bowlers, this would suit them very well.

Many commentators pointed out that a lot of runs had been scored at Edgbaston already this season, including an unbroken first wicket partnership of more than 400 for Nottinghamshire in their match against Warwickshire, but that was a little misleading, because the test match was being played on a different strip, the one that had been used for the 1999 New Zealand test, which was finished by the middle of the third afternoon.

The Toss

It has been a long-standing tradition in test cricket that the side winning the toss should bat first, but Jimmy Adams chose instead to bowl first, feeling that

33

the wicket might give a decisive early advantage to his experienced attack. In fact this was one occasion when the toss had little real significance, because Nasser Hussain wrote in a newspaper article the following day that his choice would have been to bat, so both captains had their wish.

Team Selection

England came into this match having just achieved a series win over Zimbabwe (despite some worrying moments during the second game of the two-match series), and they decided to make only one change, bringing the Glamorgan off-spinner Robert Croft back into the team for the first time for eighteen months, on the strength of his eight wickets against the West Indies at Cardiff the previous week. The fact that there were seven left-handers in the West Indian team was clearly a factor in Croft's selection, because left-handers normally have greater difficulty with a bowler of Croft's type than do right-handers.

England	West Indies
Atherton	Campbell
Ramprakash	Gayle
Hussain (Capt)	Hinds
Hick	Lara
Stewart (Wkt)	Chanderpaul
Knight	Adams (Capt)
Flintoff	Jacobs (Wkt)
Croft	Rose
Caddick	King
Gough	Ambrose
Giddins	Walsh

Umpires: D. Shepherd and
             S. Venkataraghavan

Immediate Aims

The aim of the English batsmen at the start of the innings was survival; the scoring of runs was secondary. That perhaps sounds negative or even defeatist, but in pragmatic terms it is quite justifiable, for a number of reasons:

♦   The condition of the pitch, which in the opening session at least was likely to be extremely favourable to the West Indian bowlers;

♦   The quality of the West Indian opening bowlers Walsh and Ambrose, two of the best new-ball bowlers in the world;

Robert Croft

◆ The weather was set fair, with a promise of a hot weekend to come, and batting should become much easier once the sun had dried the wicket. In consequence England would have been hoping to bat for at least an hour without losing a wicket, and would have been happy to go to lunch after two hours' play with a score of 60 for 1, which would represent a slow scoring rate, but provide a solid base for more positive batting in the afternoon session.

The West Indies, on the other hand, would be hoping for an early breakthrough; if that entailed the fall of Atherton's wicket they would be doubly pleased. Adams would feel he needed at least two wickets and preferably three in the morning session to justify his decision to ask England to bat first, and would have been happy with a lunch score of 80 for 3.

An early breakthrough was vital because his attack, with the exception of Ambrose and Walsh, was very inexperienced at this level. In the longer term he would be hoping to dismiss England for a total of between 150 and 200, whereas England would not feel happy with a score much below 300, although their recent record had been such that first-innings scores in excess of 300 were rare.

The First Day

As expected, Michael Atherton and Mark Ramprakash opened the batting for England, facing the bowling of Ambrose and Walsh. Ambrose's off-side field was that illustrated on page 25, but he moved fine-leg much deeper, pushed square-leg a little backward of square, and brought mid-on into a very close catching position – a predictably attacking field, to be followed by equally predictable accuracy. Walsh's field was almost identical, and, if he was slightly less accurate and slightly more expensive, he caused the England openers just as many problems, making the ball move either way off the seam.

Neither bowler appeared to be bowling flat out – at least the speed indicator showed they were bowling significantly below the speed achieved by the English fast bowlers against Zimbabwe. This may have been due simply to age – Walsh was 37 and Ambrose 36 – or perhaps because they each wanted to be able to bowl a long spell, but in any case their impeccable line and length more than compensated for this.

Michael Atherton

After an hour's play, however, England would have been feeling fairly happy; they had only scored 25 runs in the course of 13 overs, but no wicket had yet fallen, and, although Atherton and Ramprakash had faced considerable difficulty, their level of concentration and application had been such that no breakthrough had been achieved.

It was Ambrose who had proved more miserly where runs were concerned: five of his first six overs were maidens. Ramprakash had shown one or two signs of frustration at being unable to score off him, and even attempted to drive him back over his head in his sixth over, only to miss the ball completely. (To be absolutely fair to Ramprakash, this might also have been a counter-attack in response to Ambrose posting both a silly mid-on and a silly mid-off.) The problems posed by the two bowlers were slightly different too; Ambrose was bowling close to the stumps, nagging away on or just outside the off stump, whilst Walsh was bowling from wide of the crease, sometimes bringing the ball into the batsman, sometimes moving it away, with the occasional ball simply going straight on when it could reasonably have been expected to move like the earlier deliveries. In addition, Walsh occasionally produced a slower ball – about 67 mph rather than his normal 83 or 84.

Adams was busy in the field too, constantly making changes – he brought in a silly point when Atherton looked as if he was starting to feel comfortable playing forward to Ambrose; the object was for Ambrose to try and force him to play back and perhaps give a catch to silly point. He moved gully to a finer, fourth slip, position to stop Ramprakash playing the ball through that area – he had already scored three boundaries that way and Adams thought enough was enough.

But things were to change in the next over. After Atherton had taken a single from Walsh's first ball, a succession of very accurate deliveries at speeds varying from 67 to 84 mph had

Ambrose's field for Atherton

Ramprakash really struggling, and, misjudging the speed of the fifth ball of the over he gave a simple catch off inside edge and pad to Wavell Hinds at short-leg. This was Walsh's 450th test wicket.

Ramprakash c Hinds b Walsh 18
Atherton n.o. 4 England 26 - 1

At the other end, Ambrose was replaced by King, and at last Atherton was presented with some looser deliveries; he went on to hit four boundaries in King's first two overs, and was starting to look more convincing. But Walsh, who had very nearly bowled Hussain first ball with a superb leg-cutter when he was playing for Walsh's stock delivery which comes into the right-hand batsman from the off, continued to maintain the

Mark Ramprakash plays and misses

pressure, and another ball that jagged away took the edge of Atherton's bat, and the ball was easily caught by the wicket-keeper.

Atherton c Jacobs b Walsh 20
Hussain n.o. 1 England 44 - 2

Atherton was replaced by Hick, whose record against West Indian fast bowlers is none too impressive.

From an English point of view it was now imperative that Hick should improve on that record; from a West Indian perspective it was important that King should try harder to recreate the pressure imposed by Ambrose's accuracy.

Adams still maintained the short-leg fielder used by Ambrose and Walsh, but King was not moving the ball into the batsman in the same way. An option open to him might have been to move short-leg back to mid-on and put a man on the boundary just behind square for the pull shot which Hussain had already tried. He chose not to follow this line, however, presumably preferring to maintain the pressure imposed by having a fielder so close to the bat.

In previous series Hick had been particularly susceptible to short fast-pitched bowling, and everyone, presumably including Hick himself, was waiting for the first bouncer. Courtney Walsh, like the experienced campaigner he is, made him wait.

But off the seventh ball he received, Hick followed a wider than usual delivery without moving his feet, and edged to third slip, where the ball rebounded off the chest of Gayle to be eventually caught by Campbell fielding at second slip. England had lost their third wicket, and Jimmy Adams's decision to bowl first was vindicated.

Hick c Campbell b Walsh 0
Hussain n.o. 1 England 45 - 3

Life continued to be difficult for the batsmen in the six overs remaining before lunch, with the ball still moving a great deal off the seam, especially from Walsh, who bowled thirteen overs unchanged in the pre-lunch session. There was the occasional attempt at aggression from Stewart and Hussain, but the fact that they turned down two or three easy runs indicated that their mind was more on survival than on scoring runs.

Lunch: England 51 - 3
Hussain n.o. 2 Stewart n.o. 4

The West Indians would be feeling more than happy with that score, but conscious that Hussain and Stewart were both capable of batting for a long time. Also Knight and Flintoff were yet to come, and Knight was an experienced opening batsman, well used to being able to cope with bowlers of the calibre of Ambrose and Walsh. England would be seeking to consolidate, and aiming to avoid losing another wicket before tea.

Ambrose was now joined by yet another fast bowler, Franklyn Rose. But Alec Stewart looked particularly uncomfortable against Ambrose, and in the third over after lunch, two balls in succession jagged sharply back into him. The first beat the bat and bounced not more than an inch above the stumps; the second, almost identical but slightly fuller in length, took the edge of Stewart's bat before hitting his leg stump.

Stewart b Ambrose 6
Hussain n.o. 6 England 57 - 4

The West Indian fielders confer, alongside the wreckage of Alec Stewart's stumps

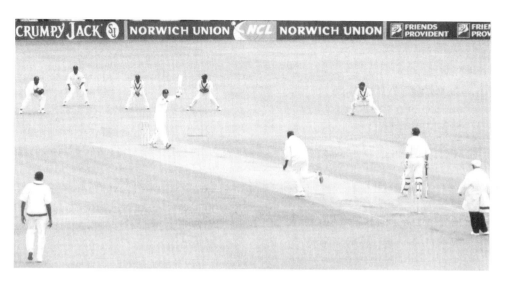

Nick Knight leaves a delivery from Franklyn Rose

Ambrose and Rose continued to bowl in tandem for a further eleven overs, and, worryingly for England, still with devastating accuracy; in one over from Rose, Knight was comprehensively beaten three times, although his wicket remained intact. Runs were hard to come by as well, Ambrose being particularly thrifty: when he was replaced by King half-way through the afternoon he had only conceded 25 runs in 16 overs, and nine of those had come in the last two overs of his spell.

The pressure on the batsmen came as much from bowling an immaculate length as from bowling a perfect line. Knight in particular had problems deciding how far to come forward, and kept being caught in his crease; an option for him might have been to stand slightly outside his crease to oblige the bowlers to reassess their length, but it takes a brave batsman to do that when faced with bowlers of the calibre of Curtly Ambrose.

Meanwhile, a stroke of bad luck awaited the England captain. Having successfully survived a ball from Rose that kept low, he was then faced with an almost identical ball which rose sharply off a length and took his glove, giving an easy catch to the keeper.

Hussain c Jacobs b Rose 15
Knight n.o. 15 England 82 - 5

The bowling of Rose and King, though still hostile and supported by the same attacking field – and much faster than that of Ambrose and Walsh – offered more scoring chances, and only four overs after the dismissal of Hussain England's score had reached three figures, helped by some quick singles and, in particular, two straight-driven boundaries from Flintoff.

Two overs later, however, Knight, trying to play more positively, drove hard at a ball from King that was much shorter and wider than most, only to see the ball fly off the edge into the safe hands of Lara at first slip.

Knight c Lara b King 26
Flintoff n.o. 16 England 112 - 6

The last thing England must have wanted at this stage was to see the world's leading wicket-taker returning to the attack, but Adams decided it was time to turn the screw, and called on Walsh for his first over of the afternoon. Flintoff played his first ball safely enough, but the second was almost a carbon copy of the ball that dismissed Atherton, and Flintoff could do no more than guide it into the hands of Lara at first slip.

Flintoff c Lara b Walsh 16
Croft n.o. 0 England 112 - 7

In the overs that remained before tea Caddick and Croft not only played sensibly but also pushed the score along, with Croft taking three boundaries off King in the final over.

Tea: England 129 - 7
Croft n.o. 16 Caddick n.o. 0

There was no real need at this stage for Jimmy Adams to do anything different, although he would have been well aware that only Ambrose and Walsh were causing real problems for the England batsmen, and that if anyone were able to survive against his two main bowlers, England could well escape from the stranglehold so far established.

For their part, with seven wickets now down, England simply needed to make as many runs as they could. Mere survival was not enough; a final score of 140 made in six hours would be no better than a score of 140 made in five hours.

But Croft and Caddick resumed after tea to find Walsh and Ambrose back in the attack, and still maintaining the line and length that had brought about the downfall of so many of their betters. It was no real surprise therefore to find Croft soon afterwards edging a ball of perfect length to Jacobs to give Walsh his fifth wicket of the innings.

Croft c Jacobs b Walsh 18
Caddick n.o. 2 England 134 - 8

Flintoff edges a catch to Lara off the bowling of Courtney Walsh

Caddick and Gough now mounted a rearguard action, and put together the biggest stand of the innings, batting aggressively but sensibly and taking boundaries from Walsh, King and Rose – but not Ambrose. At last, however, Gough stumbled as he went for a quick but perfectly safe single, and was run out at the bowler's end by a direct hit from the wicket-keeper.

Gough run out 23
Caddick n.o. 15 England 173 - 9

The innings lasted only another three overs, during which Caddick scored a further six runs, but finally Giddins, trying to hook a short ball from King, skied an easy catch to Jacobs, and England were all out.

Giddins skies a catch to Jacobs

Giddins c Jacobs b King 0
Caddick n.o. 21
England 179 all out

The West Indians were undoubtedly happier than the English with the day's play so far, although the latter may have felt very relieved to have scored as many as 179; the record of their lower-order batsmen in recent years has been such that one would not have been surprised by a score of 130 or less.

The fact that Croft, Caddick and Gough were able to make so many might have been an indication that the wicket was getting easier for batting, but more likely it was because they were for the most part facing the bowling of King and Rose rather than Walsh and Ambrose. The implication of this was that the English bowlers would have to bowl as accurately as Ambrose and Walsh if they were to dismiss the West Indies equally cheaply, because there is no doubt that it was superb bowling on their part rather than poor batting which had led to England's low score.

England would have been hoping to take at least two and preferably three wickets during the nineteen overs that remained before the close of play; the West Indies would obviously be hoping to play through that period without losing a wicket at all, but, as appears to be natural in all West Indians, they would also be hoping to have taken a substantial step towards matching England's total.

The start of the West Indian innings was encouraging for England; Gough and Caddick started bowling to an attacking field, each having three slips, two gullies, a point and a forward short-leg, the only other leg-side fielder being at fine-leg. Both bowled fast and to a reasonable length, and each began with a maiden. Caddick should in fact have had a wicket with the fifth ball of his first over, when Gayle, playing in only his fourth test, edged the ball to Flintoff in the gully, who dropped a hard but by no means impossible chance. Then in Gough's second over Campbell gave notice that he was not going to allow himself to be pinned down, scoring two from a straight drive and then three from a mistimed pull, but the fifth ball of the over beat Gayle for pace and swing and hit him on the back leg; umpire Venkat's finger was raised with no hesitation, and England had their early breakthrough.

Gayle lbw Gough 0
Campbell n.o. 5 West Indies 5 - 1

Another success could have come in Caddick's next over, when he came very close to the outside edge of Campbell's bat, but, unfortunately for England, not close enough. The next few overs were a mixture of good length, swinging deliveries and balls which were a little too wide, and Campbell and Hinds made the most of the scoring opportunities they were given, increasing the score by nineteen runs in less than four overs, but then Hinds, after hammering a ball from Caddick past mid-off for four, tried to repeat the shot to the next ball, but it was a slower delivery and he was fairly easily caught at head height by Hussain fielding at mid-on.

Hinds c Hussain b Caddick 12
Campbell n.o. 11
West Indies 24 - 2

This brought Brian Lara to the crease; if England could get him out before the close of play they would have reason to view the second day's play with a degree of optimism. But, although Lara played rather nervously, and both he and Campbell came close once or

Umpire Venkataraghavan gives Gayle out, to the joy of the English fielders

twice to losing their wicket, they not only managed to survive, but took the score to 50 before the close of play. Caddick was replaced by Giddins, who did not bowl especially well, and Gough by Croft, who bowled tidily for two overs but who did not appear to be getting any help from the wicket.

It was probably not Hussain's intention to relieve the pressure on the batsmen for the last five overs, but that effectively is what happened. He may have felt that Gough and Caddick were getting tired, but Caddick had only bowled 6 overs and Gough 8 when their respective spells ended, in other words only one more over between them than the 37-year-old Walsh had bowled on his own during the pre-lunch period. In Hussain's defence, it should be said that Giddins had bowled very well in his last test (against Zimbabwe), and if he had bowled as well on this occasion as he did then, the result might have been much more favourable. But bowling to Campbell and Lara is not quite the same as bowling to the Zimbabweans.

On balance the West Indies would be happier than England with the close-of-play position, although England would feel that a couple of early wickets the following day could well put them back in contention.

The Second Day

It was Gough and Caddick who resumed the attack at the start of the day, and the field set was a very attacking one: for Campbell Caddick had three slips, two gullies (one of them rather wider than usual, in an area where Campbell had been caught occasionally in the past) as well as a backward point and a forward short-leg. The first two overs of the day were quiet enough, but in Gough's second over Campbell showed that he was not going to allow himself to be tied down, and he hit three boundaries in five balls. Lara then hit two more off Caddick's next over, and if the first was a little streaky, the second was driven with such power and authority

Lara gets off the mark

Caddick to Campbell

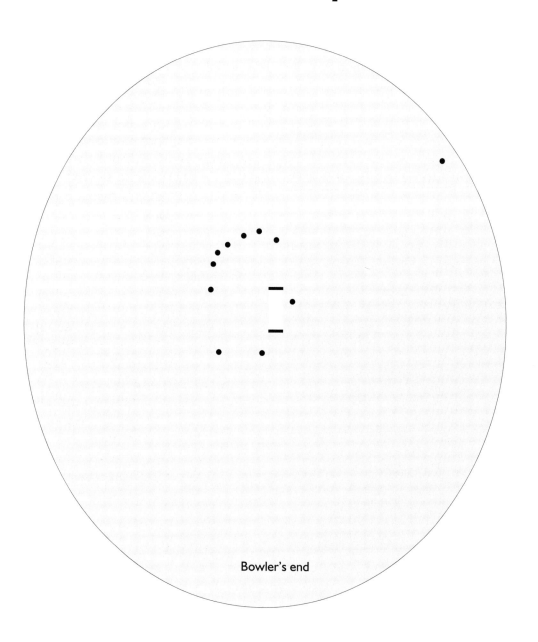

Bowler's end

Caddick's field for Campbell (right-arm fast, right-hand bat)

Campbell 31 not out

West Indies 53 - 2

that the psychological battle was already well on the way to being won by the West Indies – as was confirmed by the immediate withdrawal of Gough, England's premier strike bowler, from the attack, to be replaced by Ed Giddins.

Giddins and Caddick were ineffective, however, tending constantly to bowl too short, and by the end of the thirteenth over of the day the West Indies score had advanced to 115 for 2 – an average of five runs per over in the morning's play so far.

It was now becoming very important for England that this partnership should be broken, or all would soon be lost. The first step would be to try and put a brake on the scoring-rate (preferably by bowling the sort of line and length that Ambrose and Walsh had bowled so successfully the previous day), which would have the effect of frustrating the West Indian batsmen and perhaps encourage them to play rash shots.

Gough now returned to the attack, bowling in tandem with Flintoff, and the scoring rate now slowed considerably as they bowled a fuller length and a better line; Flintoff, indeed, began this spell with three consecutive maidens. The fuller length was especially effective against Campbell, who tends to play from the crease and so far had been allowed to do so, but now the pressure started to build as the scoring rate slowed, and the first ball of Gough's third over of this spell duly trapped Campbell in his crease and removed his off stump.

Campbell b Gough 59
Lara n.o. 42 West Indies 123 - 3

Four overs later an interesting scenario took place. Gough surprised Lara with a bouncer which he evaded, but the batsman fell over in the process. Gough then posted a man in the deep on the leg side, suggesting that another bouncer might be bowled shortly. But Gough would know that Lara is not the sort of batsman to get himself out in this fashion; he was just

No, Lara's not out – it was a bump ball!

giving him something else to think about. The second ball was a fuller length, on the leg stump, and Lara played it defensively; this was followed by a bouncer, which Lara ducked, and then by a ball just outside the off stump, which Lara attempted to drive, mis-timing the shot. This was the signal for Gough to produce a ball of perfect line and length which swung away late off the seam, drawing Lara into the shot; the ball landed safely in the gloves of the wicket-keeper having touched the edge of Lara's bat on the way through. The capture of Lara's wicket was undoubtedly a well-planned and well-executed affair, and not simply the result of one good ball coming from nowhere.

Lara c Stewart b Gough 50
Chanderpaul n.o. 5
West Indies 137 - 4

Although the West Indies were now only 42 behind England's first innings score, there was at this stage some reason for England to be optimistic. The batsmen generally perceived as representing the major threat had gone, and the West Indies were regarded as having a 'long tail', none of the four fast bowlers being considered to be great performers with the bat. Another breakthrough fairly soon could easily result in the rapid dismissal of the whole West Indies side.

So England now needed to increase the pressure if they were to get a further breakthrough. In the England innings, as soon as Knight was out, Adams had done just this by bringing on Ambrose and Walsh.

Unfortunately for England, their two most effective bowlers were already in operation. Gough and Flintoff did succeed in keeping the score down, with only 12 runs scored in the six overs that remained before lunch, but they were unable to break through.

Andy Caddick wonders what to try next

As far as the West Indies were concerned, a slow scoring rate was unimportant: even if they batted for the rest of the day and the whole of the next there would be two days left to get England out again, and what mattered now was establishing a good partnership between Adams and Chanderpaul and grinding out, if necessary, a good lead. In this they were helped somewhat by the English bowlers, especially Flintoff, because they were able to leave a high proportion of the deliveries they received, and they were never really put under pressure.

One of the problems was that Flintoff's natural ball goes away from the left-hander (and the West Indies had seven left-handers in this side). This meant that when he was bowling over the wicket, the batsman was able to leave it quite safely, and Chanderpaul in particular did this regularly. There were signs that Flintoff had realised this when he started bowling round the wicket and Chanderpaul was obliged to play, but for some reason he did not persist with this line for very long, and the pressure was taken off again.

Lunch: West Indies 149 - 4
Chanderpaul n.o. 14 Adams n.o. 3

Patient and careful batting was the order of the day for Chanderpaul and Adams in the first part of the afternoon session against the bowling of Gough, Caddick and Flintoff; when drinks were taken after an hour's play only 27 runs had been added in 15 overs, and they had still not passed England's score.

Traditionally it has been thought that frustrating West Indian batsmen in this way was a good way to ensure their early demise, but either the theory is somewhat misconceived or else Chanderpaul and Adams are not typical West Indians. The important thing for them was that they were still there, the main English bowlers were tiring, it was now hot and sunny, and they had created a good platform from which to proceed.

Adams drives Croft through the covers

An off-drive by Chanderpaul off Caddick's first ball after the resumption took West Indies past the England score, and a straight drive off the next added a further four; in fact a total of 12 runs from this first over not only appeared to signal West Indian intentions but also removed Caddick from the attack. The bowling was then shared by Croft and Giddins for eleven overs, during which time West Indies made steady, confident, but rather unspectacular progress, adding only 18 runs off 9 overs until Giddins conceded 12 in one over and was immediately removed from the attack, to be replaced by Flintoff.

The change had the desired effect, because the fifth ball of Flintoff's second over was bowled at extra pace and with extra bounce, and moved away late. Chanderpaul followed it with his bat but not with his feet, and Stewart took a very good catch.

Chanderpaul
c Stewart b Flintoff 73
Adams n.o. 25 West Indies 231 - 5

Chanderpaul was replaced by Jacobs – yet another left-hander – who quietly played out the final over before tea.

Tea: West Indies 231 - 5
Adams n.o. 25 Jacobs n.o. 1

Flintoff and Croft bowled the first two overs after tea, after which the new ball was due. Hussain a little surprisingly gave the new ball to Flintoff rather than to one of his main

The capture of Chanderpaul's wicket shortly before tea would have encouraged England. The West Indian lead of 52 was still within manageable proportions, and if they could take the remaining wickets quickly all was not yet lost; that meant, however, that they needed to take five wickets in the final session of the day. The West Indies would be aiming not only to continue batting on the third day, but also to score as many runs as possible, preferably so many that they would not have to bat a second time.

strike bowlers, presumably as a reward for taking Chanderpaul's wicket just before tea, but Flintoff proceeded to bowl most of the over wide of the off stump. Caddick then appeared to be afflicted with the same

Darren Gough

disease, with four of his first five deliveries with the new ball also passing harmlessly outside the off stump, but the sixth was a different matter entirely. It was a full length ball, on a good line, which moved away late, and Stewart took yet another catch off the edge.

Jacobs c Stewart b Caddick 5
Adams n.o. 27 West Indies 232 - 6

This brought Ambrose to the crease, and, with the remaining West Indian batsmen being specialist bowlers, England could reasonably think the end of the West Indies innings was nigh. Hussain immediately replaced Flintoff by Gough, but neither he nor Caddick was able to find the appropriate line with any degree of consistency, and the main difficulty for the batsmen came from uneven bounce, some balls keeping low and others rising alarmingly.

Hussain needed urgently to break the Adams-Ambrose partnership, and not only were his quicker bowlers proving ineffective, they were conceding runs too, so he turned to Croft's off-breaks. This move brought success with the fifth ball of Croft's second over. A lengthy conference between Adams and Ambrose had taken place after the previous ball, but whatever advice Ambrose had received from his captain, we can safely assume that it did not involve stepping right across his stumps, failing to offer a shot, and allowing the ball to hit him on the back leg right in front of the stumps. To be fair to Ambrose, the ball which dismissed him did not turn, and yet the virtually identical delivery which preceded it had turned sharply.

Ambrose lbw b Croft 22
Adams n.o. 59 West Indies 292 - 7

Croft sees yet another ball fly to the boundary

That, however, was England's last success of the day. In the overs that remained, Adams quietly progressed to 66, but Franklyn Rose set about the English bowling and scored 33 from only 32 balls, including 5 fours and an enormous six off the bowling of Croft.

Close of play: West Indies 336 - 7 Adams n.o. 66 Rose n.o. 33

With the West Indies lead now extended to 157, England's chances of winning this match had almost disappeared. Their best chance of saving the match was to take the remaining West Indian wickets quickly on the third morning, and then bat much more effectively in the second innings than in the first. There seemed little chance of their being rescued by bad weather, because the forecast suggested that it would stay hot and sunny for the remaining three days' play. There were signs too that the pitch was becoming more unpredictable, both in terms of lateral movement and bounce, and the prospects for England did not look good.

The Third Day

The weather forecast for Saturday turned out to be accurate, and the temperature was already 26°C well before play started. Adams called for the heavy roller to be used, rather than the light roller which had been used on the first two days, with a view to helping the cracks in the wicket to break up; this would tend to encourage the uneven bounce which had already been in evidence, and the West Indian bowlers, being very tall, would be able to exploit this more effectively than their English counterparts.

Flintoff and Gough opened the bowling for England, and their tactics were to attack Rose and to contain Adams; their thinking was that it would be easier to remove Rose than his captain. The theory proved correct, but by the time Rose stepped across his stumps to a Gough full toss, he had added a further 15 runs to his score.

Rose lbw b Gough 48 Adams n.o. 68 West Indies 354 - 8

Adams takes his score to 98

Rose was replaced by Reon King, whose test batting average of 1.9 suggested he would not stay long at the crease. In the event he did not improve his average, but he gave solid support to Adams, who farmed the bowling quite effectively, and he had faced 40 balls by the time Croft lured him forward with a well-flighted ball, and he was perhaps a trifle unlucky to have been adjudged out of his crease when Stewart removed the bails. He had only scored one run, but his team's score had advanced by 31, and 148 runs had been added since the first of the West Indian 'non-batsmen' had come to the crease.

King st Stewart b Croft 1
Adams n.o. 89 West Indies 385 - 9

It was now the turn of Walsh to support his captain, and he too did not let his side down, but with the score on 396, and with Adams requiring only two more runs for his century, Hussain reintroduced Gough into the attack. Walsh took a single off the second ball of Gough's first over, but three balls later Adams hit a superb cover-drive, only to see Flintoff dive to his right to take what appeared to be a quite brilliant catch, although television replays cast some doubt as to whether the ball had actually carried. So the West Indian captain was out two short of a slow but well-deserved hundred, and Courtney Walsh, by virtue of being not out for the 56th time in tests, had broken yet another world record.

As only seven minutes now remained until the scheduled lunch break, lunch was taken at this point.

Adams c Flintoff b Gough 98
Walsh n.o. 3
West Indies 397 all out

The West Indies therefore had a first innings lead of 218, far more than had seemed likely at one time, and any hopes England may have had of winning this match had gone. There was still a chance of saving the match, however, although it would take some stubborn and determined batting to pull it off.

King stumped by Stewart off the bowling of Croft

Croft to Adams

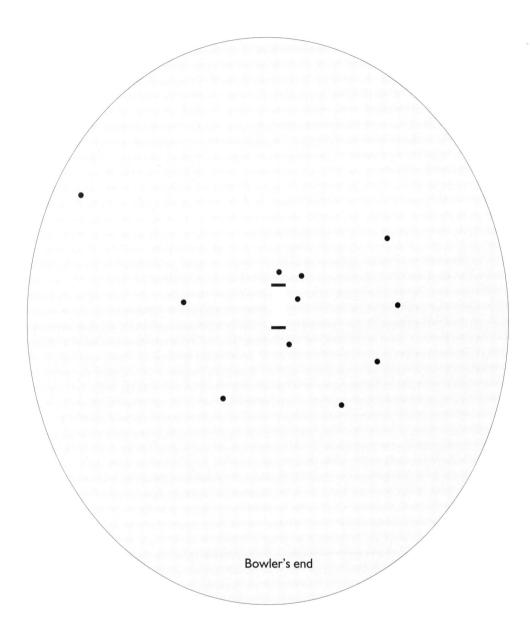

Bowler's end

Croft's field for Adams (right-arm off-spin, left-hand bat)

Adams 92 not out

West Indies 390 - 9

Two sessions of the third day still remained, and two whole days after that, and there was no sign of rain coming to the rescue. That meant a total of 240 overs had yet to be bowled, and England would need to bat for about 180 of those, and score well over 400 in order to save the match. It had been done before, of course, and everyone in the England camp could remember Atherton's match-saving 185 against South Africa at Johannesburg in 1995, and hoped against hope that history would repeat itself. Certainly a big innings was needed by someone, with solid support being offered by his colleagues, and all rash shots would have to be carefully avoided.

The West Indians, on the other hand, had all the time in the world. They could probably regard with some equanimity any England total below 400, and they were in such a strong position they would be able to afford to retain attacking fields virtually throughout the innings. If only Walsh and Ambrose could maintain the perfect line and length they had produced in the first innings, they should be able to win comfortably. They would undoubtedly be assisted by the pitch, which, now that it had completely dried out, was showing signs of cracking, so variable bounce could well be a problem.

Before a ball was bowled Ambrose walked down the pitch towards Atherton and pointedly examined the cracks just on a good length. Atherton survived the first over, albeit somewhat nervously, but in the second over Ramprakash was trapped on the back foot in front of his middle stump when a ball which pitched well outside off came back sharply into him and hit him half-way up the pad.

Ramprakash lbw b Walsh 0
Atherton n.o. 0 England 0 - 1

Ramprakash was replaced by Hussain, who, like Atherton, has on occasion been called upon to play a big match-saving innings, but his first few minutes were painful as well as uncomfortable: he was hit on the hand by a ball which bounced high off a length. He was lucky to survive a similar ball in the next over, the ball

Ambrose in action, with Hinds at short-leg

flying off the shoulder of his bat for four, although it should really have been caught at slip. The difficulty of batting was then underlined by the very next ball, which kept low; Hussain did well not only to keep it out but to send it to the boundary for another four.

It was not until Walsh's next over that the first positive attacking shot was played, Atherton clipping Walsh to the square leg boundary, but two balls later Walsh was unlucky not to claim another wicket, when Hussain played too early at a slower delivery and gave what should have been an easy catch to King at mid-off, but King declined to accept the gift.

Three maidens followed, and with both batsmen in difficulty Adams made his field even more attacking by bringing in a silly mid-off. Then Walsh produced a superb delivery, on such a line that Hussain was obliged to play it, only to see it swerve away late and take the edge of his bat; this time the catch was gratefully accepted by the wicket-keeper.

Hussain c Jacobs b Walsh 8
Atherton n.o. 5 England 14 - 2

It would not take an expert in cricket strategy to realise that the last thing England needed at this point was to lose another wicket, but very often, when your luck is out, things really go against you...

After watching Atherton survive another lbw appeal from Ambrose, and yet another ball which flew off a length and was still rising when it reached the wicket-keeper, Hick was given out caught behind for his second duck of the match. Successive replays showed that his bat did not make any contact with the ball, but there is no doubt that he was comprehensively beaten, and the ball only missed the stumps by a few millimetres.

Hick c Jacobs b Walsh 0
Atherton n.o. 5 England 14 - 3

Stewart came in and showed immediately that he was not intending to be tied down, playing two positive shots for two off Walsh. But this approach proved to be his undoing,

Atherton gets an edge to Ambrose, but survives

for, with the score on 24, he tried to cut a ball from Rose which was really much too close to cut, and merely succeeded in chopping the ball onto his stumps for the second time in the match.

**Stewart b Rose 8
Atherton n.o. 6 England 24 - 4**

With the score on 24 - 4, little more than a miracle could save England now: certainly the possibility of reaching a total of 400 seemed even further away than it had at the beginning of the innings, but at least they had two experienced opening batsmen at the crease, two men who were accustomed to being patient and dealing with the new-ball bowlers.

Batting was decidedly easier against Rose and King than against Ambrose and especially Walsh, who had so far taken 3 for 10 in 10 overs of which 7 were maidens, although there was a lot of uneven bounce, and Atherton and Knight made some progress, both playing some aggressive shots. When the score had reached 60, however, Atherton tried to cut a short, wide ball from King, but the ball kept low and he only succeeded in chopping the ball on to his stumps. It would not really have been an injudicious shot in normal circumstances, but evidence was mounting to suggest that playing with a straight bat was vital on this wicket because the bounce was becoming so unpredictable.

**Atherton b King 19
Knight n.o. 17 England 60 - 5**

That in fact was precisely what Knight and Flintoff now proceeded to do, and at tea no further wicket had fallen, but Flintoff had played two well-timed drives to the boundary.

**Tea: England 71 - 5
Knight n.o. 18 Flintoff n.o. 8**

Knight and Flintoff continued to play straight down the wicket after tea, and

Sorry reading for England supporters

a further straight drive for four by Flintoff was one of the best shots of the day, but almost immediately after, one of the fastest deliveries of the day from King kept low and removed Flintoff's off stump.

Flintoff b King 12
Knight n.o. 17 England 78 - 6

Shortly after this, Croft played a shot which would normally have been quite safe, a firmly-struck drive off his legs, only to see Wavell Hinds at forward short leg anticipate the shot, dive to his left, and hold a quite remarkable catch.

Croft c Hinds b King 1
Knight n.o. 22 England 83 - 7

Nine overs later Wavell Hinds took what appeared to be another stunning catch when Caddick edged a ball from Franklyn Rose on to his thigh, whence it rebounded to short-leg. Television replays later showed that the ball almost certainly did not carry; like Adams in the West Indies innings,

Caddick was none the less given out, and England had lost their eighth wicket.

Caddick c Hinds b Rose 4
Knight n.o. 29 England 94 - 8

But before long it was England's turn for a piece of luck, when a ball from Walsh hit Gough on the glove and was caught by Campbell at second slip, although this was adjudged to have been not out.

With the score on 111 for 8 the diet of unremitting pace was broken when Chris Gayle was brought on to bowl slow off-spin, to be joined shortly afterwards by Adams himself, bowling left-arm spin. This latter change at last brought about the demise of Knight, when a ball which had first of all hit his pad rebounded off his glove to give Hinds yet another catch at forward short leg.

Knight c Hinds b Adams 34
Gough n.o. 17 England 117 - 9

Caddick caught by Hinds off Rose

Ed Giddins – England's last man

Just why did the West Indies win? Was it superior play, superior strategy, or luck? In truth it was all three. There were undoubtedly some moments when both sides were extremely unlucky, although England's bad luck seemed to come at more crucial moments. The West Indian batting was more competent than that of England – but they did not have the bowling of Walsh and Ambrose to face. Gough bowled well, but did not get the support he needed from the other English bowlers.

Giddins very nearly provided Hinds with yet another victim off his first ball, but he then proceeded to play very sensibly in support of Gough, who was now playing quite impressively. But it was of course only a matter of time before he succumbed, and when the end came it was, fittingly, the West Indian captain who clean bowled him; the West Indies had won by an innings, and had notched up their first victory abroad since February 1997.

The turning-point of the game was undoubtedly the period following the dismissal of Lara. In recent tests the West Indian batting had been largely dependent on Lara, and his dismissal should have been the signal for England to increase the pressure. Instead of this it was the West Indies, through the determined batting of Adams and Chanderpaul who gradually turned the game around and put pressure back on England.

Giddins b Adams 0 Gough n.o. 23 England 125 all out
West Indies won by an innings and 93 runs

The West Indians celebrate their victory

Match Scorecard

England	First Innings		Second Innings	
Atherton	c Jacobs b Walsh	20	b King	19
Ramprakash	c Hinds b Walsh	18	lbw b Walsh	0
Hussain	c Jacobs b Rose	15	c Jacobs b Walsh	8
Hick	c Campbell b Walsh	0	c Jacobs b Walsh	0
Stewart	b Ambrose	6	b Rose	8
Knight	c Lara b King	26	c Hinds b Adams	34
Flintoff	c Lara b Walsh	16	b King	12
Croft	c Jacobs b Walsh	18	c Hinds b King	1
Caddick	not out	21	c Hinds b Rose	4
Gough	run out	23	not out	23
Giddins	c Jacobs b King	0	b Adams	0
Extras	lb 6, w 1, nb 9	16	lb 7, w 1, nb 8	16
Total	(69 overs, 320 min)	**179**	(58 overs, 263 min)	**125**

Fall of wickets:
First innings: 1-26, 2-44, 3-45, 4-57, 5-82, 6-112, 7-112, 8-134, 9-173
Second innings: 1-0, 2-14, 3-14, 4-24, 5-60, 6-78, 7-83, 8-94, 9-117

Bowling

Ambrose 20.5-10-32-1, Walsh 21-9-36-5, King 14.1-2-60-2, Rose 13-3-45-1

Ambrose 14-8-16-0, Walsh 19-10-22-3, Rose 10-1-43-2, King 9-4-28-3, Gayle 3-0-4-0, Adams 3-1-5-2

West Indies	First Innings	
Campbell	b Gough	59
Gayle	lbw b Gough	0
Hinds	c Hussein b Caddick	12
Lara	c Stewart b Gough	50
Chanderpaul	c Stewart b Flintoff	73
Adams	c Flintoff b Gough	98
Jacobs	c Stewart b Caddick	5
Ambrose	lbw b Croft	22
Rose	lbw b Gough	48
King	st Stewart b Croft	1
Walsh	not out	3
Extras	b6, lb 14, nb 6	26
Total	(136.5 overs, 571 min)	**397**

Fall of wickets:
1-5, 2-24, 3-123, 4-136, 5-230, 6-237, 7-292, 8-354, 9-385

Bowling:
Gough 36.5-7-109-5, Caddick 30-6-94-2,
Giddins 18-4-73-0, Croft 29-9-53-2,
Flintoff 23-10-48-1

West Indies won by an innings and 93 runs

The Second Test

Lord's

The Weather

On the morning of the first day of this, the one hundredth test to be played on this historic ground, and fifty years on from the West Indies' first test victory against England, also at Lord's, the sky was overcast, but there was no threat of rain. There was no wind, and the atmosphere was still and muggy – just the sort of day seam bowlers tend to enjoy at Lord's.

The Pitch

On the surface the pitch appeared fairly dry, with some quite rough grass, and very few cracks apparent, but footmarks revealed that there was some underlying dampness, and this, together with the weather conditions, would tend at first to favour the bowlers; in the early stages batting could be difficult.

The Lord's pitch, of course, presents one particular difficulty whatever the weather conditions: there is a considerable lateral slope. As seen from the pavilion, the pitch slopes steeply from left to right – in fact there is something like a three metre drop from one side of the ground to the other. That means that a straight ball bowled from the Pavilion end will tend naturally to swing in to the right-hander and away from the left-hander, whilst a straight ball bowled from the Nursery end will swing in to the left-hander and away from the right-hander. It is not only the batsman who can be troubled by this, however: bowlers too can find it difficult to control their line until they become accustomed to these unusual conditions.

The Toss

Alec Stewart, standing in as captain for Nasser Hussain, out of the match with a broken thumb, won the toss and, not surprisingly when one considers the conditions, decided to bowl first. Jimmy Adams said in an interview that he was quite happy with that situation, because the pitch looked pretty good, but, given his bowling strengths and the fact that his normal tendency seems to be to ask the opposition to bat first, it would have been surprising if he wouldn't really have preferred to have Ambrose and Walsh opening the proceedings.

Team Selection

West Indies only made one change to the victorious Edgbaston side, Adrian Griffith replacing Chris Gayle (one left-hander coming in to replace another). England made a number of changes, with Michael Vaughan replacing the injured Nasser Hussain, Dominic Cork replacing Croft, and two more Yorkshiremen, Craig White and Matthew Hoggard coming in for Flintoff and Giddins respectively. England therefore had no regular spinner (although Hick and Vaughan bowl occasionally) but included five seamers.

England	West Indies
Atherton	Campbell
Ramprakash	Griffith
Vaughan	Hinds
Hick	Lara
Stewart (Capt & Wkt)	Chanderpaul
Knight	Adams (Capt)
White	Jacobs (Wkt)
Cork	Rose
Caddick	King
Gough	Ambrose
Hoggard	Walsh

Umpires: S. Venkataraghavan and J. Hampshire

The Natwest Media Centre at Lord's, seen from the Pavilion

Immediate Aims

For West Indies it was essential for their openers to cope successfully with a swinging ball and establish a base for a big score. For England on the other hand, an early breakthrough was important if they were not quickly to lose hope of squaring the series. Both teams would be aware that a West Indies win would effectively kill the series stone dead: it is extremely difficult to win a five-match series if one loses the first two games.

The First Day

Both sides began in attacking mode. Gough had an especially attacking field; when bowling to Campbell he had three slips, two gullies, a point and a forward short-leg, but, unusually, there was no fielder on the off-side between point and the bowler. The West Indian opening batsmen were not intimidated, however, and they scored 14 off the first two overs. What is more, they appeared willing to take risks too, but unfortunately for England the chances they gave either did not go to hand or were dropped: off the ninth ball of the match Campbell played a ball from Caddick uppishly on the off side to see it drop just short of Vaughan in the gully, and seven overs later the same batsman edged the ball to Cork at third slip, but the chance was missed. It would in truth have been an extremely good catch, but no harder than many others seen in this and other series.

When Gough gave way to Hoggard the West Indies had already scored 40 without loss from ten overs. Both Gough and Caddick had struggled to find a length, and, contrary to expectations, the ball had not swung to any significant degree. Hoggard's first over - his first in test cricket - was extremely impressive, as was the rest of his spell, and he was unfortunate not

The West Indians doing their warm-up exercises before the start of play

to have any success. Dominic Cork replaced Caddick at the Nursery end, and immediately found the edge of Griffith's bat, only to see White at third slip miss the opportunity. Again it would have been a good catch, but not an unduly spectacular one. In the same over the West Indies reached 50 without loss: they had required only 56 balls and 54 minutes to reach this mark.

Against the bowling of Cork and Hoggard, however, the scoring rate slowed - in fact after the 50 was reached only seven more runs were scored in the next 44 balls. During this time Campbell was again extremely lucky, edging a ball from Cork into the slips where Hick at second slip dived across Atherton, who seemed poised to take a straightforward catch, and appeared to knock it from his hands. Very soon afterwards two drives and a square cut from Campbell each found the boundary, and the West Indian opener went to 51 out of a total of 72.

White replaced Hoggard and Caddick replaced Cork, but lunch arrived without further incident and, more importantly for the West Indies, without a wicket being lost.

There was no doubt that the English bowlers had not used the conditions as well as they might - one suspected that Ambrose and Walsh would have made considerable inroads into the English batting if they had bowled first. True, there had been some good bowling, but it had been inconsistent, and the batsmen were never under real pressure. In addition three definite chances had been dropped, and as a result England were now on the back foot, and West Indies were on the way to building a good total despite having been asked to bat first.

Lunch: West Indies 79 - 0
Campbell n.o. 53 Griffith n.o. 26

Music added to the carnival atmosphere before the game and in the intervals

What were England to do? Clearly Gough and Caddick, as the two main strike bowlers, needed to bowl with more discipline, but also the England fielders needed to be more alert and take whatever chances came their way; in test cricket such chances tend to be few and far between.

So far the West Indian batsmen had been positive but rather lucky; if straightforward chances had been taken they could easily have been 79 for 2 or worse, and if the English bowlers had taken those wickets they might very well have been spurred to bowl better. If the luck turned England's way things could look very different, but in truth it was already starting to look like a repeat of Edgbaston.

The umpires: John Hampshire (left) and Srinivasaraghavan Venkataraghavan

In the event England did not have long to wait for a stroke of luck. Gough opened the afternoon session with a well-directed bouncer which Griffith did well to evade. His second ball was turned to fine leg. As the batsmen turned for a second run, television commentator Richie Benaud made a comment he would probably prefer to forget: "the running between wickets has been very good today"; Caddick threw a magnificent return to Stewart, who removed the bails with Griffith still a foot or more short of his crease.

Griffith run out (Caddick) 27
Campbell n.o. 53 West Indies 80 - 1

Griffith was then replaced by another left-hander, Wavell Hinds. Gough (and the rest of the England fielders) were convinced that he was out caught at the wicket early in his innings; not until after they had finished celebrating did they think to turn round to look at umpire John Hampshire, who had given him not out – quite rightly, because, as the replay showed, the ball had come off Hinds' arm, not his glove.

After ten overs White took over from Gough, and again luck was with Sherwin Campbell, when he came within inches of playing the ball onto his off stump. Caddick and White now tried all they could: Caddick had four men on the boundary, two on the leg, two on the off, but Campbell refused the invitation to play a hook or a lofted drive. They tried bouncers, yorkers, slower balls, bowling round instead of over the wicket, but all to no avail, although there were some very close leg before wicket appeals. The ball was swinging a little more now, with an occasional hint of reverse swing.

Cork then replaced Caddick, and Michael Vaughan took over from White, bowling slow off-spin. Vaughan bowled two tidy overs, but then two successive boundaries took Hinds to his half-century, and West Indies to 162 for 1.

The question might have been asked: why not bring Matthew Hoggard into the attack? He had bowled well in the morning, admittedly with no success, but none of the other bowlers had taken a wicket either. Presumably Stewart thought the introduction of a slow bowler would ask new questions of the batsmen, which is always a good thing to do, but it made some people wonder why England had included five pacemen in their line-up if they were not going to use them.

But if Hoggard was not bowling, he was very soon in the action in a different way. Campbell at last accepted an invitation to hook Cork, and Hoggard took a good catch at long leg.

Campbell c Hoggard b Cork 82
Hinds n.o. 50 West Indies 162 - 2

Even though they had just taken a second wicket, Stewart's decision to bowl first was now looking to be a trifle misguided, especially since the wicket was playing quite well. The West Indies were in a very strong position, and looked set for a big score, probably in excess of 400, which would probably be enough to ensure that England could not win the game. With a batsman like Lara coming to the crease at 162 for 2 the game could easily go right away from England, and it was even more important than usual to get Lara out early.

The West Indian players' balcony

With only four overs to go before tea Lara and Hinds were content to play quietly, and when the interval came, a total of 92 had been scored in the session at a rate of more than three an over.

Tea: West Indies 170 - 2
Hinds n.o. 55 Lara n.o. 2

Gough and Cork bowled the opening overs after tea. Cork was bowling very aggressively, and the ball was swinging more than it had earlier in the day. Cork's aggression also appeared to have a positive effect on Gough – or perhaps it was the stimulus of bowling against Lara that made him start bowling faster. Lara showed that he is still a force to be reckoned with by playing a magnificent square cut to the boundary off the bowling of Gough, but on the third ball of Gough's next over he flashed at another ball outside off without moving his feet, and Stewart took a good catch off the outside edge.

Lara c Stewart b Gough 6
Hinds n.o. 56 West Indies 175 - 3

However overjoyed England might have been at the early dismissal of Lara, the arrival of Chanderpaul, who along with Adams had batted the West Indies into a winning position at Edgbaston, would have warned them that there was still a lot of work to do. Cork's continued aggression, this time as fielder rather than bowler, very nearly brought another run out, but after a further two overs the weather had become rather gloomy, and the West Indian batsmen accepted the umpires' invitation to leave the field. The England players were not happy, because they felt they were starting to get back into the game, but there was nothing they could do about it.

Fortunately the bad light was not the prelude to rain, and it was possible to resume play forty minutes later.

When play did resume, Gough and Caddick continued their attack, and three overs later their aggression was rewarded, albeit as a result of an umpiring error. After a succession of short deliveries Cork pitched the ball up to Hinds, who had batted beautifully up to this point. No doubt expecting yet another short-pitched

Cork and Caddick examining the ball

ill Hinds played from his crease instead of getting forward, and appeared to edge the ball to Stewart. In fact successive replays showed that no contact was made with the bat, but of course the umpire has to make a decision on what he sees, without the benefit of endless replays; Hinds was given out, and Cork had taken his 100th wicket in test cricket.

Hinds c Stewart b Cork 59
Chanderpaul n.o. 7
West Indies 185 - 4

Unfair as it may seem, such strokes of luck can sometimes turn games, and the West Indians might well have felt a little aggrieved; yet they know, as all cricketers know, that it is in the nature of the game for such errors to be made, and most professional cricketers will say that these things tend to even themselves out over time.

Be that as it may, the West Indian captain now arrived to join Chanderpaul, and England, well aware of what this pair had been able to achieve in the Edgbaston test, were determined to prevent a similar partnership from developing. In fact Adams was lucky to survive his first two deliveries from Cork, and a single from a push on the off side brought him to face Gough, who immediately brought in a third slip. The third ball of the over pitched on leg stump and straightened; Adams was trapped in front of his stumps, and England had the wicket they most prized after that of Lara. Moreover there was no element of luck about this one.

Adams lbw b Gough 1
Chanderpaul n.o. 7
West Indies 186 - 5

Two overs later Hoggard relieved Gough, but was much less impressive than in his first spell, conceding 33 runs in six overs. Cork, however, was as

England on the attack

miserly at the other end as Hoggard was generous. The ball was now swinging more than it had all day, which presented Stewart with something of a problem because the new ball was due shortly — should he take it and risk losing the effect of swing? In the event the decision was virtually made for him; with two overs to go before the new ball was due Jacobs attempted to hook a bouncer from Cork but could only glove it to the wicket-keeper.

Jacobs c Stewart b Cork 10
Chanderpaul n.o. 18
W. Indies 207 - 6

This was followed two overs later by Ambrose giving a bat/pad catch to Ramprakash off the fifth ball of an over during which the West Indian fast bowler had been all at sea.

Ambrose c Ramprakash b Cork 5
Chanderpaul n.o. 19
West Indies 216 - 7

Bill Frindall, *Test Match Special*'s statistician

The situation had thus changed dramatically. Largely because of the eight overs Cork had bowled since the resumption after the bad light break, during which he had taken 3 wickets for only 13 runs, Stewart's decision to bowl first now looked almost justifiable, and the West Indians were the ones who had now been forced on to the back foot.

Stewart decided to delay taking the new ball – after all, his bowlers could hardly do better with the new ball than they were currently performing with the old one – and Hoggard and Cork concentrated their attack on Franklyn Rose. They let Chanderpaul take a single early in Hoggard's next over, and let Rose keep the strike by giving him a single off the last ball; in Cork's next over they allowed Rose to take two when only one would normally have been possible. They clearly felt that Rose was there for the taking, especially given his tendency to move across his stumps before the ball was bowled. But Rose retaliated in the best way possible. After ducking two bouncers from Hoggard he hooked the next ball for six, then hit two fours and a two on the leg side, taking 16 off the over and advancing his side's score to 241 for 7.

This was the signal for Stewart to take the new ball, but Rose immediately clubbed Caddick for a straight four. (In fact it was intended to be a pull, but it was hit so hard that it was just as effective as if it had been properly timed.) He then hit Gough to the mid-on boundary, but finally played and missed, to the relief of all the television and radio commentators who had been saying he was "an lbw waiting to happen". But by that time he had scored a very valuable 29 off 29 balls, and had saved the West Indian innings from total collapse.

Rose lbw b Gough 29
Chanderpaul n.o. 21
West Indies 253 - 8

Rose's replacement, Reon King, also thought that attack was the best tactic, and he too hit Gough to the boundary. But in the meantime Shivnarine Chanderpaul had been starved of the ball. In the last thirteen overs he had only faced seventeen balls, and now, facing the bowling of Gough, he failed to get to the pitch of a good length ball and succeeded only in edging the ball on to his middle stump to give another important boost to England's counter-attack.

Chanderpaul b Gough 22
King n.o. 4 West Indies 258-9

Courtney Walsh avoided his habitual duck by taking a single off his first ball from Gough with a straight drive, whereupon King hit two boundaries from the last two balls of Gough's over, so it was something of a surprise when, with only four balls left of the scheduled play for the day, the umpires decided the light was too bad for play to continue, and led the players from the field.

Close of play: West Indies 267 - 9
King n.o. 8 Walsh n.o. 1

The English close fielders, always ready

A score of 267 was certainly higher than England would have wished at the start of play, but bearing in mind that the West Indies had at one time been 175 for 2, they must have been mightily relieved. Adams would no doubt have been disappointed that his side had not capitalised on their good start, but would also feel that the score was not so low that they were in imminent danger of defeat; on the contrary, he would feel that anything Cork and Gough could do, Ambrose and Walsh could probably do better. In hindsight, though, he might also have felt some relief that England had not held their catches in the morning session; the West Indian position could then have been extremely precarious.

How had England managed to get back into a match that had seemed to be going away from them? Partly, it has to be said, through luck, especially where the dismissal of Hinds was concerned; partly through tactics, especially that of preventing Chanderpaul from getting a sight of the ball; but most of all from the sheer determination of Dominic Cork, who had taken four wickets himself, bowling with tremendous aggression. Moreover this aggression had rubbed off on to Gough, who as a result also ended the day with a four-wicket tally.

The Second Day

The remainder of the West Indian innings did not take up much of the second day – Walsh was trapped leg before off the first ball of the day, a full length delivery from Caddick.

Walsh lbw b Caddick 1
King n.o. 12 West Indies 267 all out

There was now renewed speculation as to what the great West Indian bowling combination of Ambrose and Walsh would do on this pitch, particularly bearing in mind that some rain had fallen during the night and the atmosphere was more humid than on the previous day; conditions could not have been better for seam bowling. In addition, the memory of the English batting crumbling in the face of this attack at Edgbaston was only too vivid.

Curtly Ambrose

Although 267 was not a very high score, England's first innings record in the past two or three years did not make their supporters feel confident that they could surpass this score and perhaps establish a good first innings lead. The first hour's play would be crucial; if they were able to survive the first hour in such difficult conditions, then a platform might be established on which they might build, but much depended on the England openers Atherton and Ramprakash.

The first ball from Ambrose gave little inkling of what was to come; given just a little width outside the off stump, Atherton played the ball confidently past point for a single. But Ambrose never needs much time to find his optimal line and length, and with the last ball of his first over, which pitched on or fractionally outside off stump and swung away late, he had Ramprakash caught by Brian Lara at first slip off the outside edge; it was Ramprakash's second duck in succession.

Ramprakash c Lara b Ambrose 0
Atherton n.o. I England I - I

In recent years England supporters had needed to clutch at any straw, and they would certainly feel that if a wicket had to fall at that stage, they would prefer it to be that of Ramprakash rather than that of Atherton, who was renowned for his patience and had a proven track-record of playing long and obstinate innings. But on this occasion that optimism was misplaced, for, exactly six balls later, with the final ball of Walsh's first over, Atherton attempted a forcing shot outside the off stump to a ball which he should have left; more to the point it was a very poorly executed shot, and Lara was able to take an even easier catch than the one he had taken a few moments earlier.

Atherton c Lara b Walsh I
Vaughan n.o. 0 England 2 - I

Psychological warfare

If Ramprakash's recent record in tests had been poor, Graham Hick's was even poorer: he had been dismissed for a pair at Edgbaston. But Hick survived the opening salvos, and it was Vaughan who, after being dropped in the slips by Campbell, was dismissed by Ambrose, who was now bowling beautifully. A ball which pitched on the off stump found its way between bat and pad and Vaughan was out bowled, beaten for pace by a near perfect delivery.

Vaughan b Ambrose 4
Hick n.o. 1 England 9 - 3

England's start could hardly have been worse, but some relief was to come when Walsh was removed from the attack after an opening spell of five overs, to be replaced by Franklyn Rose. At last English supporters had something to cheer, as Graeme Hick proceeded to take 17 runs from Rose's first over, driving and cutting four times to the boundary with great authority; a score of 30 for 3, however bad, looked much less depressing than 13 for 3, as it had been only six balls earlier!

Hick also dispatched Curtly Ambrose to the cover boundary with equal authority, but Ambrose detests giving away singles, let alone boundaries, and he took his revenge by bowling a ball which pitched on the off stump and came sharply into Hick, taking the inside edge before hitting the top of the stumps; Graeme Hick's aggressive resistance was over.

Hick b Ambrose 25
Stewart n.o. 3 England 37 - 4

Shortly after this Stewart edged a ball from Rose into the slips, where to the relief of all except the West Indians Lara dropped a fairly straightforward chance, and when Ambrose was replaced by King there was a feeling that if England were going to stage a recovery, now was the time. Although Rose was now bowling better than in his initial over to Hick, there was no doubt that once Walsh and Ambrose left the attack, batting was a much easier proposition. At this point Ambrose had taken 3 wickets for 17 runs in 9 overs, including 4 maidens.

But Knight never really looked comfortable, and after playing an extraordinary shot to a short delivery from King which flew high in the direction of fine leg but fortunately for him fell safely to ground, he steered another ball from the same bowler into the slips, where Campbell made amends for having dropped Vaughan.

Knight c Campbell b King 6
Stewart n.o. 9 England 50 - 5

Graeme Hick

Knight was replaced by Craig White, and England still needed nine runs to avoid being asked to follow on, but Stewart, who was now playing very confidently, took the eye with two drives to the boundary, one square, the other almost straight, off the bowling of Rose, and the lunch interval was reached with no further alarms for the England dressing-room. Of the 58 runs so far scored, 32 had come off the bowling of Rose; without that profligacy England's plight could very well have been even worse than it was. The follow-on had technically not yet been avoided, but even the most

Alec Stewart's favourite shot

pessimistic English or the most optimistic Caribbean supporters now had that in mind.

Lunch: England 58 - 5
Stewart n.o. 17 White n.o. 0

During the pre-lunch period Ambrose had done the bulk of the bowling, whilst Walsh had only had one short spell. Adams now continued his tactic of bowling one of his experienced players at one end and a less experienced bowler at the other, but a boundary by White in King's first over followed by another by Stewart off the first ball of Walsh's new spell saved England from the embarrassment of having to follow on, and then Stewart pulled King for an all-run four. King was tending to ball too wide and too short, and the pressure on the England batsmen was clearly easing as Stewart and White played confidently and correctly, scoring 21 in the first eight overs after lunch. But no batsman can ever feel totally comfortable or confident when facing Walsh, and with the score on 85 Walsh angled a ball in to Stewart which he was obliged to play, but late swing took the edge and Jacobs took the catch.

Stewart c Jacobs b Walsh 28
White n.o. 16 England 85 - 6

Stewart's replacement, Dominic Cork, was extremely lucky not to follow suit off the very next ball, but soon three boundaries, two from White and one from Cork, took the England score into three figures. But then a badly judged run from a shot played to Jimmy Adams at short cover led to Craig White being easily run out by a direct hit from the West Indian captain. It was an unnecessary dismissal, the shot being played firmly straight to Jimmy Adams' throwing hand.

White run out (Adams) 27
Cork n.o. 4 England 100 - 7

Whether Cork's concentration was disturbed as a result of running out White when he was batting so well it is difficult to say, but in the following over he too was back in the pavilion, having tried to drive a ball from Walsh and just getting the faintest of outside edges, to give the West Indian wicket-keeper yet another catch.

Cork c Jacobs b Walsh 4
Caddick n.o. 0 England 100 - 8

A few minutes later, at 2.55 pm, the umpires decided that the light was too bad for play to continue, and led the players from the field. Sensibly, they decided to take tea at 3.10 pm instead of 3.40, and it was possible to resume play at 3.30 pm.

With only Gough, Caddick and the debutant Matthew Hoggard remaining to face the devastating accuracy of Ambrose and Walsh, it seemed that the England innings would soon be over. But that is not how the batsmen in question saw it; Gough, indeed, had the temerity to hoist Walsh high over the mid-wicket boundary for six. Caddick had a couple of lucky escapes, twice edging into the slips only for the ball to fall short of the waiting fielders, but also playing a controlled shot for four down to third man. Eventually, however, he too fell victim to Walsh's persistent off-stump line and was caught by Campbell at second slip, but

The English batsmen under siege

he had helped Gough to add eighteen useful runs.

Caddick c Campbell b Walsh 6
Gough n.o. 9 England 118 - 9

If Hoggard felt nervous as he came to the crease to face his first ball in test cricket it did not show when he pulled Ambrose to the leg-side boundary to open his account. It was an ungainly shot, but effective, and the English resistance was to last a further 23 minutes, with 16 runs added before Gough went the way of so many before him, caught at first slip off the bowling of Ambrose.

Gough c Lara b Ambrose 13
Hoggard n.o. 12
England 134 all out

The first three overs of the West Indian second innings were fairly uneventful, but in the next over, with the score 6 for 0, Caddick bowled a short delivery wide of the off stump

England therefore had amassed almost exactly half of the West Indian total, and there were still three days left to play, in addition to what was left of the extended post-tea session of the second day. Their only hope as far as winning the game was concerned was to dismiss the West Indies fairly cheaply and hope their batsmen would be able to achieve the target set; if they got West Indies out for 100, then they would have plenty of time to score the 234 needed for victory. But the omens were not good, and even a draw looked unlikely at this stage.

As far as the West Indies were concerned, they simply needed to keep their heads and play sensibly; if they batted until the end of the third day they would set England an impossible target, and they would have two days to dismiss a side whose totals in the series so far had been 179, 125 and 134. Indeed there was a fair chance that they had enough runs in the bank already.

Darren Gough before the game

which Campbell smashed high over gully, only to see Gough racing round the boundary from third man to take a stunning catch.

Campbell c Gough b Caddick 4
Griffith n.o. 1 West Indies 6 - 1

Not only was this a vital catch, it was so sensational that it could not fail to inspire, and two balls later another wicket fell. Another short-pitched delivery from Caddick reared up at

Hinds, and then looped up to short leg, where Ramprakash claimed the catch. To the naked eye and at normal speed it looked out, and umpire Hampshire thought so too; it needed a number of slow-motion replays to show that Wavell Hinds had now been given out caught twice in the match without having touched the ball: it had actually touched the top of his arm and then his helmet before rebounding into the hands of Ramprakash.

Hinds c Ramprakash b Caddick 0
Griffith n.o. 1 W. Indies 6 - 2

Gough also made the ball bounce, and Griffith too was hit on the helmet, though with rather less unfortunate consequences. But shortly after, he got the finest of edges to a good length ball from Darren Gough, and he too was on his way back to the pavilion.

Griffith c Stewart b Gough 1
Lara n.o. 0 W. Indies 10 - 3

Lara and Chanderpaul looked at first as if they would steady the innings, but then Lara fended off a beautiful delivery from Caddick, and Cork took a straightforward catch in the gully.

Lara c Cork b Caddick 5
Chanderpaul n.o. 9
West Indies 24 - 4

This brought Jimmy Adams to join Chanderpaul, and one's thoughts went back once more to Edgbaston. The West Indian innings was in disarray, but even with the score on 24 for 4, they still had a lead of 157, and these were the two batsmen who were likely to be the most difficult to dislodge.

But luck was on England's side, and once more the West Indians were on the wrong end of an umpiring mistake, when umpire Venkataraghavan gave Chanderpaul out, caught once more by Ramprakash at short leg, when the ball had actually hit his hip rather than his bat.

Chanderpaul c Ramprakash b
Gough 9
Adams n.o. 0 West Indies 24 - 5

There is no doubt that England had been extremely lucky over the dismissals of Hinds and Chanderpaul, but it was a matter of fact that Gough and Caddick were bowling like men possessed, and all the English fielders were on their toes. In these conditions there is no guarantee that Hinds and Chanderpaul would have gone on to

A stunning stop by Cork – but not a catch

Caddick to Lara

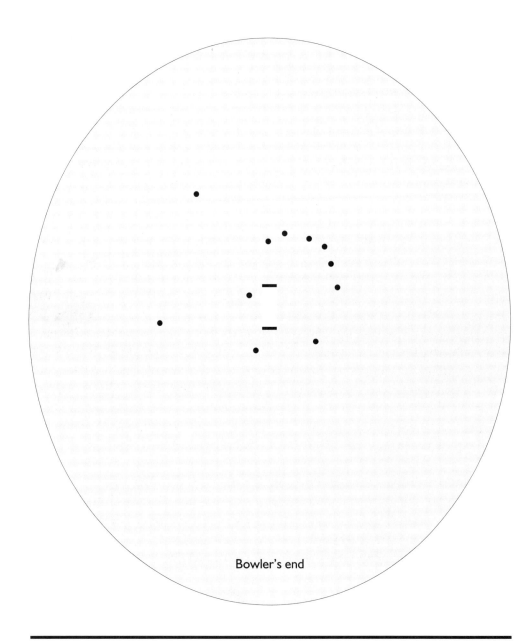

Bowler's end

Caddick's field for Lara (right-arm fast, left-hand bat)

Lara 5 not out

West Indies 24 - 3

make runs anyway. As for the 30,000 spectators, they may not have been on their toes, but they were certainly on the edge of their seats.

Ridley Jacobs was lucky not to be out early in his innings when he edged a ball hard and high to Knight in the slips. Knight got a finger to it, but the ball went for four. Furthermore, in trying to take the catch, Knight had broken his finger.

Jacobs now decided to go for his shots, the plan being that Adams would play an anchor role at the other end, and he played one delightful shot to the cover boundary off Gough.

Then for a moment Caddick (and everyone else) thought that he too had given a catch to Ramprakash, but the English celebrations were short-lived: umpire Hampshire considered that the ball had hit his hip not his bat, and television replays this time proved the umpire to have been correct. Soon afterwards, however, he went to drive a good length ball from Caddick, and

Ramprakash takes a catch – or does he?

the ball flew off the edge of his bat into the hands of Atherton at first slip.

Jacobs c Atherton b Caddick 12
Adams n.o. 3 West Indies 39 - 6

This was a very important wicket for England to take, because the way Jacobs was swinging at the ball, only a few lusty blows would have been needed to put the West Indies out of England's reach. As it was, the remaining West Indian batsmen were all capable of putting bat to ball, and there was much for England still to do.

One of the things they had to do was continue putting the ball in the right place, and Caddick in particular did exactly that. With the West Indian total still on 39, he trapped Adams leg before with a ball that pitched just outside off and came in sharply, and then Ramprakash took yet another catch at short leg when Ambrose fended off another rising ball.

Adams lbw b Caddick 3
Ambrose n.o. 0 West Indies 39 - 7
Ambrose c Ramprakash
b Caddick 0
Rose n.o. 0 West Indies 39 - 8

A few balls later Ramprakash very nearly took another catch, diving full length as King fended off a ball from Caddick, but this time he could not quite get his fingers to it. By this time Cork had replaced Gough, and he also bowled in a very hostile fashion, and it was no great surprise when he too found himself among the wickets, taking a straightforward return catch from Rose when the batsman tried to turn him to leg and only succeeded in getting a leading edge.

Rose c & b Cork 1
King n.o. 1 West Indies 41 - 9

Walsh came in – for the second time in the day! – determined to hit as hard and as high as he could, but he was unable to find the boundary; in fact the only time the ball reached the boundary at this stage of the proceedings was when a bouncer from Caddick hit King on the helmet and went for four leg-byes.

The resistance was not long-lasting, however, and Cork finished off the innings by trapping King in front of his stumps; England had stuck to their task, and the West Indies had been dismissed for 54.

What was interesting was that Alec Stewart gathered his team around him for a few minutes before leading them from the field to great acclaim. Obviously he wanted not only to ensure that everyone in the team knew what the approach was to be, and that before the current euphoria had subsided, but also he wanted the public to be aware of the determination to which the calling of this team-talk bore witness.

King lbw b Cork 7
Walsh n.o. 3 West Indies 54 all out

So England had bowled out West Indies more cheaply than they had ever done before in the whole history of the game; in fact only against Australia in 1999 (51 all out) and Pakistan in 1986 (53 all out) had West Indies scored fewer runs for the loss of all ten wickets.

The scoreboard at the end of the West Indies second innings

So what had brought this about? And what part did strategy have to play in these dramatic events? In truth, it has to be said, not a lot. From a West Indies standpoint it would clearly not have been their intention to be dismissed for 54, so whatever their game-plan was, it was either not implemented or it simply didn't work.

As far as England are concerned, we have already seen that they could not afford to lose this match, and that if they did not dismiss West Indies cheaply they almost certainly would lose. The motivation for doing well was therefore very strong, and this may have been helped by a certain degree of complacency on the part of the batting side, who already had a lead of 133 and who, even after being dismissed for 54, were now asking England to do better in their second innings than they had done in the whole series so far.

Motivation, of course, is not enough, but it does thrive on success, and the earlier that success comes, and the more sensational its form, the more motivated does the side become. From this point of view Gough's catch in the deep was a turning-point. Sheer good luck plays its part too, and most of the luck that was going went England's way, especially the umpiring decisions. Once wickets started falling it was quite easy to maintain an attacking field; in fact in the circumstances Alec Stewart really had no alternative. But the way Caddick and Gough, and in the later stages Cork, first of all found and then maintained the ideal line and length, that is what really guaranteed the success.

In other words, what was demonstrated here is that ultimately it is performance, not strategy, that achieves success. Admittedly, if the strategy is wrong success will not come, but if the players do not perform, strategy alone will not do the job.

Some of the euphoric England supporters

But, for all this talk of success, England so far had only done half the job; there was still the little matter of 188 runs to score to level the series at 1 - 1.

Moreover eight overs remained until close of play; it was clear to everyone that if England lost even one wicket during that remaining session the balloon was likely to burst and their chances of winning would be seriously damaged. That is why we were treated to the unusual spectacle of a Lord's crowd cheering the umpires when they decided that the light was too bad to allow play to continue and took the players off after only seven balls had been bowled.

**Close of play: England 0 - 0
Atherton n.o. 0 Ramprakash n.o. 0**

The Third Day

At the start of the day the West Indies would be feeling fairly confident. If the pitch was as responsive to fast bowling as it had been the previous day, in Ambrose and Walsh they had the bowlers to exploit it. Moreover they had recent experience of defending a small total: only four months previously, in Trinidad, they had dismissed Zimbabwe for 63 when only 99 were needed for victory. They could afford to maintain an attacking field for a considerable time – certainly until lunch, or even well into the afternoon.

England could afford to take their time to a certain extent; they had two whole days in which to make the 188 runs required. The reality, though, was that they needed to bat all day. If they did that, they would almost certainly get the runs; by coincidence, 188 runs was exactly the number scored on the second day even though 21 wickets had fallen. On the other hand, not many of the English batsmen had shown themselves capable of withstanding Ambrose and Walsh for long periods, so occupation of the crease with no thought of pushing the score along might be a risky option. But even Ambrose and Walsh are human and need to rest occasionally; at least they should be able to score runs from the support bowlers. The key to it all, however, seemed to be Michael Atherton. As long as Atherton was around, England had a chance; if he went early, the signs would not be good.

Radio and TV commentator Barry Richards

When the time came for play to begin on the Saturday morning, rain was falling. Fortunately it did not last long, and play began only fifty minutes after the scheduled starting-time. Tension was high all around the ground, and even seemed to affect Courtney Walsh, who opened the morning's play and England's account with a no-ball.

But it was Walsh who drew first blood. As Ramprakash tried to play a forcing shot into the covers off the back foot, he found the ball coming back into him, and he merely succeeded in playing it off the bottom edge onto his middle stump.

Ramprakash b Walsh 2
Atherton n.o. 0 England 3 - 1

Atherton was joined by Vaughan, who is actually more accustomed to opening an innings than Ramprakash, and the two of them set about establishing a platform for the England innings. Atherton was certainly in no hurry, and it was over half an hour before he opened his account; the roar which greeted that quick single was scarcely exceeded by those which subsequently greeted a boundary to third man (from a shot very similar to the one which had brought about his downfall in the first innings) and a hook to the mid-wicket boundary from another Walsh no-ball.

The contest was hotting up, one felt, but then the weather intervened once more, and the players left the field because of rain at 12.30. Sensibly lunch was taken at once, which meant that no playing time was actually lost.

Lunch: England 13 - 1
Atherton n.o. 9 Vaughan n.o. 0

The interval gave Ambrose and Walsh a chance to have a little rest, so they were able to continue when play resumed. After Atherton had taken a streaky four through the slips off Walsh (he had been trying to turn it to leg), Walsh was convinced he had Vaughan caught at the wicket, only for umpire Hampshire to turn down the appeal. There had certainly been a distinct

The scene at Lord's at 11 am on the third day

noise as the ball passed the bat, but the television replay showed that the sound was of bat hitting pad, and the umpire's decision was correct. Vaughan celebrated by driving Walsh back down the ground for three; he was finally off the mark after facing 29 deliveries.

This was a fascinating period of play, with the West Indian bowlers bowling well and the English batsmen matching them. Every run had to be fought for, and was loudly cheered, especially when first Atherton and then Vaughan pulled Ambrose to mid-wicket and mid-on respectively.

Eventually some relief came in the shape of a change of bowling. Even Walsh cannot go on for ever, and when Rose took over, life became a little easier for the batsmen, and both of them dispatched him to the boundary. Very soon their partnership had reached the fifty mark; it had taken 77 minutes, which, given the situation and the quality of the bowling, represented a fairly healthy scoring rate.

Ambrose, however, was being as miserly as ever, but Atherton and Vaughan were now feeling secure enough to consider ways of putting him under pressure and disturbing his rhythm: they started taking quick singles at every conceivable opportunity, although it has to be said that they did not get many such opportunities. Rose at the other end continued to be rather profligate (he conceded 36 runs in eight overs,

compared with Curtly Ambrose's 13 from 13 overs), but he was unlucky at one point when Atherton played a defensive shot which then bounced over his stumps as he looked everywhere to see where it had gone.

But as the quick singles and boundaries kept coming, so the balance seemed to be changing, and when England were half-way towards their target of 188, Atherton and Vaughan were still together. Walsh, however, was now back in the attack, and he had other ideas. He bowled a good length ball to Vaughan which pitched just outside off stump and held its own instead of coming back down the hill; Vaughan edged it to the wicket-keeper.

Franklyn Rose

Walsh's reaction was more exhortatory than celebratory: he was clearly trying to motivate the rest of the team to finish off the job he had started.

Vaughan c Jacobs b Walsh 41
Atherton n.o. 39 England 95 - 2

Hick immediately cut Walsh for four, and then a single from Atherton took England into three figures: 88 runs still needed. Hick's intentions were clearly to be as aggressive as possible, especially against the support bowlers, and the luck was with him. When he tried to clip a ball from King to square leg he was missed at short leg by Hinds, who had only just been moved there for that very purpose. Hick celebrated his good fortune by hooking Walsh's last ball before tea for four.

Tea: England 109 - 2
Atherton n.o. 44 Hick n.o. 9

With only 79 now needed to win and eight wickets in hand, the odds had now shifted in favour of England, and all they needed to do was keep their heads and carry on as before. The problem facing Adams was much more tricky:

♦ His side could not win if they didn't take eight more wickets;

♦ If they wanted to take wickets they needed to maintain an attacking field;

♦ If they maintained an attacking field they would give runs away more quickly.

Quite apart from all that, there had been a light shower of rain during the tea interval, and the outfield was therefore a little damp; that meant that as soon as the ball travelled along the ground it would pick up moisture, perhaps soften, and become more difficult for the bowlers to control.

Atherton and Hick return to the crease after tea

Ambrose to Atherton

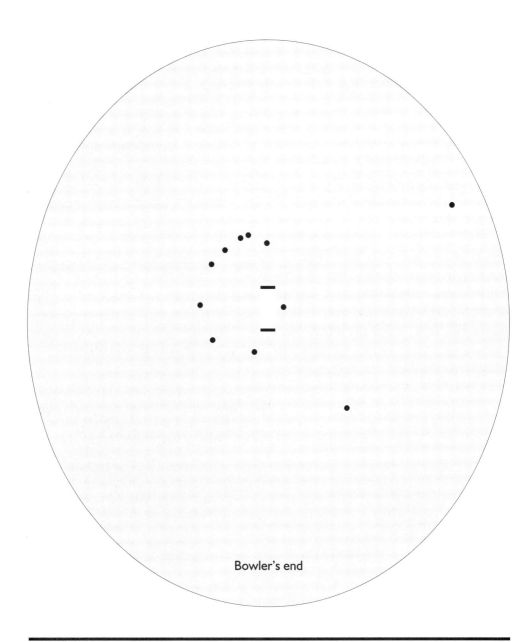

Bowler's end

Ambrose's field for Atherton (right-arm fast, right-hand bat)

Atherton 44 not out

England 109 - 2

In reality there is only one option when you have Ambrose and Walsh; that is to maintain the attack, and that is what Adams did, with Ambrose now bowling from the Nursery end to three slips, a short leg, a backward point and a short cover.

It was soon clear that the only thought in Ambrose's mind was all-out attack; the fourth ball of his first over lifted sharply and jammed Atherton's finger painfully against the bat-handle. But it was still something of a cat-and-mouse game too, as was shown two balls later when Ambrose quite deliberately bowled wide of the off stump, inviting Atherton to try again the shot that had got him out in the first innings; Atherton declined the invitation.

Walsh started his first over after tea with a no-ball, and the next ball was hammered by Hick through the covers for four. Then a series of quick singles meant that eight runs had been conceded in the one over. For some reason Walsh did not have a short leg in position as did Ambrose, and that is what enabled the English batsmen to make so many runs in that over.

Then a chance was missed which could have proved expensive. Hick edged the first ball of Ambrose's next over to third slip, where Chanderpaul failed to hold the catch. Hick was showing a tendency to stay back in his crease, only moving forward to a full length ball after playing his shot, and that is why he edged the ball in that way – he had done exactly the same thing in the first innings, and also in both innings at Edgbaston. Bowlers like Ambrose and Walsh take note of such things, and it was no great surprise when, in Walsh's next over, Hick did exactly the same thing once more and was caught at first slip by Lara.

Hick c Lara b Walsh 15
Atherton n.o. 45 England 119 - 3

Stewart, who replaced Hick, played the first ball he received down to third man for a single, but off the very next ball Atherton was lbw to a ball from Walsh that was significantly faster than most of those he had bowled. Walsh had now taken four wickets for 45 runs.

Atherton lbw b Walsh 45
Stewart n.o. 1 England 120 - 4

Atherton: disappointed and disbelieving

With those two quick wickets and two new batsmen at the crease, one of whom, Knight, was batting with a broken finger, the odds were shifting once more in favour of the West Indians. But Knight and Stewart are both accustomed to opening an innings, and therefore not unused to facing Walsh and Ambrose; as before they just needed to keep their heads. The West Indians now had their tails up; Stewart and Knight must make sure they went down again.

The next few overs were quiet affairs, with very few runs being scored and no particular alarms for the English batsmen, even when Rose replaced Ambrose. Stewart had clearly modified his technique for this innings, moving across for each delivery so as to have a better chance of hitting it down the ground; in this way he reduced the risk of giving a slip catch, but increased the chance of being out leg before, but, given the way the ball was bouncing, that risk was diminished anyway.

Then Rose's inexperience began to show. A ball which pitched short was dispatched to the leg boundary, between mid-wicket and mid-on, with Stewart's characteristic pull shot. Rose retaliated with a bouncer so high that not only could Stewart afford to ignore it completely, but even a batsman of Curtly Ambrose's stature would have needed an extra long bat in order to reach it; for some reason it was not called as a wide. The next ball Stewart pulled once more to the leg-side boundary – a carbon copy of the shot he had played two balls earlier.

Once more the balance seemed to be turning, especially when Walsh appeared to be having some difficulty with his line during the next over; was the great man getting tired? If so, was Ambrose yet ready to come back, or would the pressure now be taken off England by the introduction of another bowler?

Walsh himself soon provided the answer. The second ball of his next over kept low, and Alec Stewart was

Courtney Walsh

hit on the pad, incontrovertibly out leg before wicket.

Stewart lbw b Walsh 18
Knight n.o. 2 England 140 - 5

Suddenly the 48 runs still needed for victory seemed a colossal target, but there was still no need for any change of approach by either side, although English players and supporters must have been wishing that Walsh's 37 years were weighing a bit more heavily on his shoulders and that he would soon be replaced.

Craig White now came in to face Walsh, and edged his first ball to Lara at first slip, who claimed the catch, but then said he was not sure if it had carried. The matter was referred to the third umpire, and there was some confusion as the screen which conveys the decision to both players and crowd indicated first of all that he was both out and not out simultaneously. Eventually the replay showed that the ball had in fact bounced well in front of Lara, and the correct decision was made. The next ball from Walsh was a bouncer which White did well to evade. Then came a peach of a ball which beat White completely and went between bat and pad; wicket-keeper, slips and bowler all appealed for a catch, umpire Venkataraghavan allowed the appeal, and Walsh now had six wickets. Only afterwards did the replay show that the ball had touched White's shirt, but not his bat.

White c Jacobs b Walsh 0
Knight n.o. 2 England 140 - 6

Cork survived a double appeal off his first ball, one for lbw, the other for a catch at short leg, but the ball was clearly missing leg stump, and his bat was a long way away from the ball; but English hearts were in mouths.

Then Knight appeared to edge the first ball of Rose's next over to Jacobs, who failed to take the catch; perhaps to his relief, the replay showed that Knight had not in fact made contact anyway.

Knight was now tending to ignore anything bowled outside his off stump. Normally one would expect him as the senior batsman to take the initiative in

How did you survive that one?

this situation, but the way he was holding his bat suggested that the broken index finger on his right hand was making it difficult for him to play attacking shots. The West Indian tactic was now for Rose to bowl defensively and for Walsh (and, presumably before much longer, Ambrose) to take a more attacking line at the other end.

Walsh was now bowling to Cork. Cork played and missed two or three times, but then launched into a fierce cover drive, which sent the ball speeding to the boundary. This was immediately followed by a straight drive which did not reach the boundary, but the batsmen managed to run four anyway.

If those two shots relieved the pressure somewhat, bringing the number of runs needed by England below 40, the next over from Rose put the pressure on again. After four dot-balls, Rose produced a full length ball which Knight at last tried to drive, but he did not really move his feet, the ball moved away off the seam and he played inside it, giving Jacobs a straightforward catch off the thinnest of edges.

Knight c Jacobs b Rose 2
Cork n.o. 8 England 149 - 7

Caddick survived the last ball of Rose's over, and then it was Cork's turn to face Walsh again. The first ball of the over brought an lbw appeal, but the ball was easily missing leg stump. Then Cork took a quick single, which brought huge cheers, and the England

The West Indians celebrate Knight's dismissal

score to 150. Caddick then took another quick single, off the edge, but safe, and another over from Walsh was survived.

That the pressure was just as great for the bowlers as the batsman was demonstrated by Rose's next over. Caddick square cut the first ball, pitched too short and too wide, for four, then came the predictable bouncer. Then after one straight ball and another bouncer came a no-ball, a ball bowled so wide that one wondered why it was not called as such, followed by a similar one which was.

Ambrose then replaced Walsh, and now the problems of field-placing in this situation really were coming into play. Short leg had been moved back onto the boundary, which meant that Cork was able to take a quick single off a thick edge played on the leg side.

Dominic Cork

Then for Caddick Adams brought in an extra slip and moved square leg over to the off side, which meant Ambrose was now bowling to a 7/2 field. Normally this would not be a problem for a bowler as accurate as Ambrose, but it meant that when he bowled a perfectly straight delivery, Caddick was able to take two runs to mid-wicket.

Two lights now appeared on the bad-light indicator, but Alec Stewart, from the players' balcony, mouthed instructions to the England batsmen to stay in the middle even if the light were offered. The reasoning was perfectly clear: any break in play would give Ambrose and Walsh a rest, and they would be able to come back refreshed and bowl in tandem, in which case England's chances of scoring the remaining runs would be greatly reduced. It was perhaps slightly risky, asking non-specialist batsmen to face Ambrose and Rose (who had bowled faster than anyone else in the match so far) in fading light, but it was understandable.

Two balls later, however, Caddick missed a ball from Ambrose and he was out leg before wicket; Ambrose, who had bowled beautifully throughout the innings, had at last taken a wicket. Such was the delight of Ambrose's captain that he not only hugged his bowler, but picked him up, no mean feat considering the relative size of the two men!

Caddick lbw b Ambrose 7
Cork n.o. 10 England 160 - 8

When Cork faced Rose in the next over he made his intentions quite obvious – it was to be all-out attack. After playing and missing at the first two balls, and clipping the third off his legs for two, he pulled the fourth over mid-wicket into the stand for six, swung and missed at the fifth, and then played a lofted on-drive for four off the final ball of the over. Twelve runs from the over, and sixteen to win.

Having played a big part in getting England back into the match it was clear that Dominic Cork was not going to let it all slip away.

But Ambrose had other ideas, and continued to bowl as tightly and as aggressively as ever, but Gough's solidly correct forward defensive shot drew almost as many cheers as had Cork's six in the previous over. Three lights were now showing on the light meter, but Cork and Gough were not going to let that distract them. A close shout for lbw by Ambrose against Gough concentrated minds somewhat. Ambrose was bowling just as well as he had been throughout the innings, but when he produced a perfect yorker Gough produced an equally perfect defensive shot to keep it out – it was a riveting battle.

Such runs as did come came slowly, Ambrose bowling two more maidens. Walsh returned to the attack for a final burst, conceded four runs in one over but could easily have had a wicket or two. Then Cork played an uppish drive off Ambrose towards Jimmy Adams at mid-off. Adams dived forward but was about six inches short of being able to catch it; miraculously he still held on to the ball and prevented a single. Cork was hit first on the arm, then on the fingers, and both batsmen came close to being run out. The activity and excitement of the whole game seemed to be encapsulated in these final overs.

Cork attacks Rose

Eight overs after Caddick's dismissal, with the score on 185 for 8, Cork tried to turn Walsh off his legs; he missed with his bat, but the ball went off his pads into the vacant area between square-leg and fine-leg, and had to be fielded by the wicket-keeper. The result was two leg-byes, and the scores were level. For a while the scoreboard showed 186 for 8, but eventually, to the accompaniment of tremendous cheers, it was corrected to 187 – only one run was needed to win, and the fielders all moved in to save any single being taken.

Alec Stewart after the match

Three balls were delivered from Walsh which were as testing as any he had delivered all day. Finally, off the fourth ball of the over, Cork smashed a square drive to the boundary, the match was won, and the series levelled at one match apiece.

England 191 - 8
Cork n.o. 33 Gough n.o. 4
England won by 2 wickets

Alec Stewart receives the winner's cheque

So ended an extraordinary match. As former Australian captain Richie Benaud said 'I don't think I've ever seen anything like this, and I've been fiddling around with this game for quite some time...' If ever it was necessary to stage a match which demonstrated to what extent cricket is a psychological just as much as a physical game, this would be the one. It was a game which on the first day looked to be won by the West Indies only for England to fight back; a game in which at lunch on the second day the situation was such that the London evening papers had banner headlines 'Pathetic England'; one which at tea on the final day looked to have been won by England, but in which the issue was really in doubt right until the final over.

It was also a game keenly fought, with no quarter asked or given, but played without sledging or unpleasantness, and one where great performances were acknowledged by the players, from whichever side they came. As if to symbolise it all, Dominic Cork, who won the Man of the Match award, waited for Curtly Ambrose and presented him with one of the two stumps he had carried off the field. In short, it was one of those games which no one who was there, whether player, commentator or spectator, will ever forget.

Needless to say, England's heroics had once more prompted people to say 'Is this the great revival at last?'

Match Scorecard

West Indies	First Innings		Second Innings	
Campbell	c Hoggard b Cork	82	c Gough b Caddick	4
Griffith	run out	27	c Stewart b Gough	1
Hinds	c Stewart b Cork	59	c Ramprakash b Caddick	0
Lara	c Stewart b Gough	6	c Cork b Caddick	5
Chanderpaul	b Gough	22	c Ramprakash b Gough	9
Adams	lbw b Gough	1	lbw b Cork	3
Jacobs	c Stewart b Cork	10	c Atherton b Caddick	12
Ambrose	c Ramprakash b Cork	5	c Ramprakash b Caddick	0
Rose	lbw b Gough	29	c and b Cork	1
King	not out	12	lbw b Cork	7
Walsh	lbw b Caddick	1	not out	3
Extras	b1, lb 8, w2, nb 6	13	lb8, nb1	9
Total	(89.3 overs, 384 min)	267	(25.4 overs, 128 min)	54

Fall of wickets:
First innings: 1-80, 2-162, 3-175, 4-185, 5-186, 6-207, 7-216, 8-253, 9-258
Second innings: 1-6, 2-6, 3-10, 4-24, 5-24, 6-39, 7-39, 8-39, 9-41
Bowling:
Gough 21-5-72-4, Caddick 20.3-3-58-1
Hoggard 13-3-49-0, Cork 24-8-39-4
White 8-1-30-0, Vaughan 3-1-10-0

Gough 8-3-17-2, Caddick 13-8-16-5
Cork 5.4-2-13-3

England	First Innings		Second Innings	
Atherton	c Lara b Walsh	1	lbw b Walsh	45
Ramprakash	c Lara b Ambrose	0	b Walsh	2
Vaughan	b Ambrose	4	c Jacobs b Walsh	41
Hick	b Ambrose	25	c Lara b Walsh	15
Stewart	c Jacobs b Walsh	28	lbw b Walsh	18
Knight	c Campbell b King	6	c Jacobs b Rose	7
White	run out	27	c Jacobs b Walsh	0
Cork	c Jacobs b Walsh	4	not out	33
Caddick	c Campbell b Walsh	6	lbw b Ambrose	7
Gough	c Lara b Ambrose	13	not out	4
Hoggard	not out	12.	(Did not bat)	
Extras	lb 5, nb 3	8	B3, lb 8, w 1, nb 12	24
Total	(48.2 overs, 225 min)	134	(69.5 overs, 263 min)	191- 8

Fall of wickets:
First innings: 1-1, 2-1, 3-9, 4-37, 5-50, 6-85, 7-100, 8-100, 9-118
Second innings: 1-3, 2-95, 3-119, 4-120, 5-140, 6-140, 7-149, 8-160
Bowling
Ambrose 14.2-6-30-4, Walsh 17-6-43-4
Rose 7-2-32-0, King 10-3-23-1

Ambrose 22-11-22-1, Walsh 23.5-5-74-6
Rose 16-3-67-1, King 8-2-17-0

England won by 2 wickets

The Third Test

Background

Five weeks had elapsed since the dramatic events of the Lord's Test, during which time the two sides joined with Zimbabwe in competing for the Natwest one-Day Trophy, ultimately won by England. This Third Test, when it finally came, was redolent with significance: from the point of view of the series, both sides would be anxious to avoid defeat at all costs, because the side that lost this match would be obliged to win the two remaining games in order to win the series. From an England point of view, there was a widespread eagerness to see whether their resurgence would be maintained. Finally, this match would see the 100th appearance of those two English stalwarts and former captains, Alec Stewart and Michael Atherton.

The Weather

Except for a few days here and there, the weather had not significantly improved since Lord's. It was perhaps a little warmer than it had been earlier, but as the third test approached the weather deteriorated, and heavy rain at Manchester during the previous two or three days, followed by further rain during the night immediately prior to the match meant that the outfield was quite wet, and there were even some muddy patches on the square; fortunately the weather forecast was reasonably optimistic for the remainder of the match.

A delayed start was inevitable: after a pitch inspection at 11 o'clock it was decided that, if no further rain fell, play would commence at 12 noon.

The Pitch

The pitch looked dry on top, but there appeared to be some dampness under the surface. The Old Trafford pitch tends to be abrasive, causing the ball to wear quickly, and often causing reverse swing when the ball is about 40 or 45 overs old, which would favour the England bowlers Gough and White. Spin too, often plays a part at Old Trafford, so England would be expecting Croft to play an important part in this match.

Team Selection

England made a number of changes from the team which had won at Lord's, some of them as a result of

Coach and captain:
Duncan Fletcher and Nasser Hussain

what had happened in the One-Day tournament, some as a result of recovery from injury. Hussain was now fit to return, replacing Nick Knight and taking over the captaincy once more; Marcus Trescothick, fresh from his one-day success, was brought in to make his debut, replacing Ramprakash; Graham Thorpe came in for Graeme Hick and Robert Croft replaced Matthew Hoggard, the expectation being that spin would play a part in this test, at least in the later stages.

England	West Indies
Atherton	Campbell
Trescothick	Griffith
Hussain (Capt)	Hinds
Thorpe	Lara
Stewart (Wkt)	Adams (Capt)
Vaughan	Sarwan
White	Jacobs (Wkt)
Cork	Rose
Croft	Ambrose
Caddick	King
Gough	Walsh

Umpires: P. Willey & D. Cowie

The Toss

West Indies won the toss, and Jimmy Adams decided (contrary to his normal practice) to bat first, saying that he liked the look of the surface. Nasser Hussain said he too would have chosen to bat given the chance, but he did feel there would be something in it for the bowlers in the early stages. Adams' decision to bat first could have been influenced by the fear that on the last day the pitch might turn a lot, and

Robert Croft would perhaps be as effective against them as he had been for Glamorgan earlier in the season. Whatever Adams' reason may have been, former West Indian fast bowler Ian Bishop, now a television commentator, said he 'nearly fainted' when hearing of the decision.

Immediate Aims

England would be hoping to dismiss West Indies for under 200 if possible, and certainly try to restrict them to a score lower than 250, West Indies would be hoping for a score of more than 300. With the series now level at 1 - 1, each side needed to treat this as the first game in a three-match series.

With play starting late, with only one hour's play due before lunch, England needed to get out of the blocks early, preferably taking two wickets before lunch; three would put them well on top. The West Indies would be aiming to make a solid start, and not lose any wickets during the initial one-hour session.

The First Day

The match got off to a quiet start. It was clearly not a wicket with a lot of pace in it, but both Gough and Caddick were able to make the ball swing to a significant extent, Caddick in particular swinging the ball both ways. But it was Gough who struck first: with the fourth ball of his second over Gough found the edge of Campbell's bat and

the ball was very well taken, low down at third slip, by Thorpe.

Campbell c Thorpe b Gough 2
Griffith n.o. 0 West Indies 3 - 1

The umpires: Peter Willey and Doug Cowie

Three overs later Griffith was defeated by swing, this time by Caddick, and he was trapped lbw right in front of his middle stump.

Griffith lbw b Caddick 2
Hinds n.o. 6 West Indies 12 - 2

This was precisely the start England wanted, and they continued pressing, coming close to dismissing both Hinds and Lara, and Lara had faced eighteen balls before he finally got off the mark with a boundary to third man off Gough. A few minutes later light rain began to fall, and the teams left the field five minutes before the time scheduled for lunch.

Lunch: West Indies 21 - 2
Hinds n.o. 10 Lara n.o. 4

After lunch England would need to press home their early advantage. Getting Lara out would be their prime objective, but they would also be well aware that Hinds had so far under-achieved in this series, and they needed to ensure that this was not the occasion for him to come good. For their part West Indies would not be too depressed, but would want to make sure that no further wickets fell during the course of the afternoon. It would, however, be unlikely that Hinds and Lara would show the kind of patient application displayed by Adams and Chanderpaul in the Edgbaston Test; the likelihood would be that if no further wicket fell before tea the score would have advanced into three figures, which would represent a much more acceptable start. If that were to happen, England would feel the initiative had been wrested from them.

Only 26 balls into the session rain intervened once more. No further wicket had fallen in that time, and Hinds and Lara had added six runs to the total, including three from a good-looking off-drive from Hinds off Gough, which in normal circumstances would have easily reached the boundary; today, though, the outfield was much slower than usual because of the damp conditions. More significant in this period, however, was the frequency with which the ball had passed the bat outside off stump; neither batsman had appeared confident against the swinging ball.

Rain break: West Indies 27 - 2
Hinds n.o. 15 Lara n.o. 5

The delay lasted almost twenty minutes, but after the resumption only the remaining four balls from Caddick's over and the first two balls of a new spell from Cork were possible, with no addition to the score, before the rain arrived again, this time more heavily than before.

Rain break: West Indies 27 - 2
Hinds n.o. 15 Lara n.o. 5

The centurions: Atherton and Stewart

Although Cork completed his unfinished over on the resumption, he was immediately replaced by Darren Gough. At the other end Caddick was having great difficulty with his run-up: large quantities of sawdust had been used to fill holes made in the damp turf, and Caddick felt the ground was slipping away beneath his feet as he ran in. Hinds made the most of this, and hit him for two boundaries with a confidence which he had not shown earlier.

Gough continued to cause problems at the other end, and was unlucky not to get the wicket of Hinds with a slower ball which turned off the pitch; Hinds had intended to hit it to leg but mistimed the shot, and it ballooned into the air off the leading edge. Croft ran towards it from mid-off only to see it fall to the ground inches in front of him. To make things worse for the batsmen, there were also signs in this over that reverse swing was already beginning to come into play.

Caddick was then replaced by Cork, who opened with a maiden – largely because nearly every ball was well wide of the off stump and the batsman did not offer a shot. The first ball of his next over was also much too wide, but the second came very close to the outside edge of Hinds' bat. The next ball was virtually identical, but this time umpire Cowie adjudged the bat to have made contact and he gave Hinds out caught at the wicket. Hinds would appear to have been the victim of a bad decision for the third time in three

innings, but two balls later Jimmy Adams appeared to benefit from compensatory generosity when the same umpire gave him not out when Cork appealed for leg before.

Hinds c Stewart b Cork 26
Lara n.o. 13 West Indies 49 - 3

In Gough's next over, however, England got the wicket they really wanted, when Lara played at a ball just outside off, opening the face of the bat and giving a catch to Thorpe at third slip: the third time in this series that he had been dismissed by Gough in similar fashion.

Lara c Thorpe b Gough 13
Adams n.o. 0 West Indies 49 - 4

Michael Vaughan
throws in from the boundary

Cork to Hinds

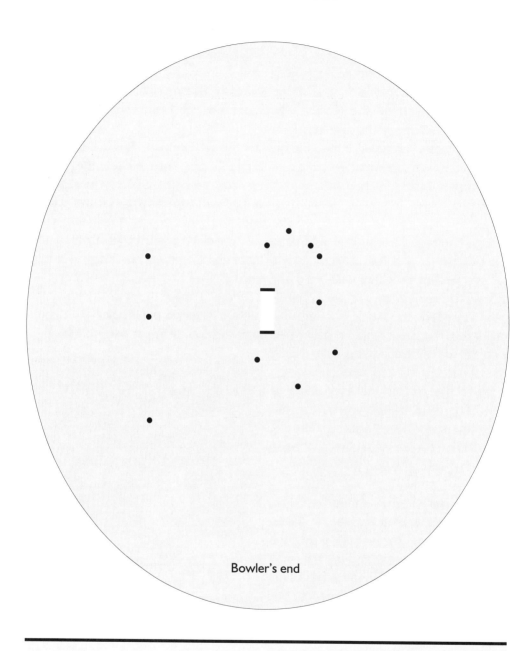

Bowler's end

Cork's field for Hinds (right-arm fast-medium, left-hand bat)

Hinds 26 not out

West Indies 49 - 2

The loss of these two wickets meant that West Indies now needed to concentrate hard to ensure that no further wicket fell before the close of play, but it also gave them the opportunity to unsettle the English bowlers a little by rotating the strike; so far the bowlers had maintained a good line against the left-handers, and now for the first time there was a right-hand / left-hand combination.

Adams and the young Sarwan proceeded to bat circumspectly but with confidence after Adams had edged a ball from Gough through the slips to the boundary, and the score mounted slowly but steadily. Caddick replaced Gough with the score on 61 for 4, and he and Cork bowled until the close of play with continued aggression. Sarwan was dealt a painful blow on the arm by a short no-ball from Caddick, and then played another no-ball from Caddick to the third-man boundary. Adams played a confident cover-drive for four off the bowling of Cork, and was nearly brilliantly caught at forward short-leg by Vaughan when playing an equally confident shot to leg during Cork's final over of the day. But close of play came at 7.15 pm, and West Indies had achieved their objective of surviving without further loss.

Close of play: West Indies 87 - 4
Adams n.o. 16 Sarwan n.o. 17

The Second Day

At the start of the second day the West Indian captain must have been feeling that there was still a lot of work to be done if he were to be able to justify opting to bat first on this pitch, although it has to be said that the way he and Sarwan batted in the final session of the previous day's play suggested that it was indifferent batting rather than a devilish pitch that had caused his side to slump to 49 for 4. At any rate the matter was to a certain extent in his own hands, and he and the 20-year-old Sarwan needed to make sure that they batted for the greater part if not all of the pre-lunch session.

Friday was a cold day for everyone –
especially slip fielders

Darren Gough opened the attack, and there was an early alarm for the West Indies as Sarwan fended the ball uppishly as it rose into his ribs, but fortunately for him there was no fielder near enough to take the catch. Sarwan also looked uncomfortable in Gough's second over when the ball caught the bottom edge of his bat when he was in the act of withdrawing it, but again the ball fell safely to ground, and two balls later he put all that behind him as he drove the same bowler past point for four.

In the meantime, at the other end, Adams too was having a torrid time against Caddick, first of all being struck in the stomach by a ball that he decided to leave alone, and then having an extraordinary piece of luck when he played the ball on to his stumps but the bails failed to fall. Then in the following over, after a rising ball struck him on the thigh pad and went for four leg-byes to bring up the fifty partnership and the West Indian hundred, he was hit in the stomach once more, this time by Gough.

But after nine overs without a wicket falling, Hussain decided on a double bowling change, with Dominic Cork coming on to replace Caddick and Craig White to replace Gough. These two bowled three overs each before the players stopped for a drinks break, during which time twelve runs were scored but no wicket fell, although Sarwan was badly hurt by a fast ball from White which hit him in the chest; it was later revealed that he had cracked a rib.

It often happens that a break of some kind, whether for drinks, rain, lunch, tea, etc. will break a batsman's concentration, and so it proved this time, for Cork's first ball after the break was a perfectly straight ball

Sarwan is hit in the ribs by a delivery from Craig White

which pitched on the stumps and Sarwan missed. Cork appealed in his usual dramatic fashion, and umpire Doug Cowie upheld the appeal. Undoubtedly this was a big blow for the West Indies, but at least after a partnership of 69 their position was looking a good deal healthier than it had when Sarwan came to the crease.

Sarwan lbw b Cork 36
Adams n.o. 21 West Indies 118 - 5

Sarwan was replaced by Ridley Jacobs, who immediately showed aggressive intentions, though, at least to begin with, without tangible result, as he either played and missed or drove straight at a fielder; when he did finally reach the boundary it was as a result of an outside edge running between the slips.

Hussain clearly felt that it was a good idea to rotate his bowlers on a regular basis, and after Cork had bowled three overs he called on Caddick once more. With the first ball of his new spell Caddick achieved what Cork and White had nearly done, but not quite: he bowled a yorker at the West Indian wicket keeper, who played and missed, turning round to see his off stump flattened.

Jacobs b Caddick 7
Adams n.o. 22 West Indies 126 - 6

Franklyn Rose replaced Jacobs, and hit Caddick for four wide of mid-on, although not exactly in classic fashion. Then in the following over, White bowled an away-swinger just wide of Adams' off stump, and the West Indian captain played at it, only to give

Jimmy Adams caught by Thorpe off Caddick

Ridley Jacobs bowled by Caddick

Graham Thorpe in the slips his third catch of the innings.

Adams c Thorpe b White 22
Rose n.o. 4 West Indies 130 - 7

The West Indian innings was now in some disarray, and with batsmen such as Rose and Ambrose at the crease there was only one way to go, and that involved hitting the ball hard – which both of them have proved themselves to be capable of doing on a number of occasions. But this time it did not work, at least not for Ambrose; Caddick bowled slightly wide of off stump, and Ambrose pulled the ball round hard in the direction of mid-wicket. Normally it would have been a certain four runs, but instead Hussain took a brilliant catch, and it was the English fielders who were celebrating rather than the West Indian batsmen.

Ambrose c Hussain b Caddick 3
Rose n.o. 6 West Indies 135 - 8

Rose was now joined by Reon King, and this pair added another thirteen runs before lunch, including six to Rose off one ball from Caddick: the ball was flicked towards Vaughan at deep square leg, and, on receiving Vaughan's return Alec Stewart tried to throw down the stumps at the bowler's end, only to see the ball fly straight past the stumps and cross the boundary rope at the far end.

Lunch: West Indies 148 - 8
Rose n.o. 16 King n.o. 2

Once more an interval proved to be a batsman's undoing, and yet again it was Dominic Cork who profited; once more his first ball after the break, full and straight, hit Rose on the pads, right in front of the stumps – Rose's normal method of dismissal – and the West Indian resistance was almost over.

Rose lbw b Cork 16
King n.o. 2 West Indies 148 - 9

But Courtney Walsh was determined not to give his wicket away without a fight, and equally determined to score some runs in the process. He took a single from Cork off his first ball, and twice hit Gough for three in the following over, before being deceived by the first ball of Cork's next over and being rapped on the pads. So preoccupied was he with the business of scoring runs that he was too busy telling his partner not to run for a leg-bye to notice that the umpire's finger was raised.

Walsh lbw b Cork 7
King n.o. 3 West Indies 157 all out

This was the sort of result Nasser Hussain might have hoped for if he had won the toss and invited his opponents to bat first, but hardly what Jimmy Adams had in mind at the start of the first day's play. England had bowled themselves into a very strong position, but there must always be a feeling that, whatever any other bowlers can do on a given wicket, Ambrose and Walsh are likely to be able to match. The big question mark here would be to what extent the other bowlers would be able to back them up; so far in the series they had signally failed to do so. As always they would be hoping for an early break, and would very much like that to include the wicket of Atherton, but on this occasion, with such a small first-innings total to defend it was even more crucial.

A typically dramatic appeal from Dominic Cork as he traps Franklyn Rose leg before

When the England innings began Curtly Ambrose opened the bowling, and Michael Atherton opened the England account by taking a single down to fine leg. Marcus Trescothick, in his maiden test innings, played out the rest of the over without scoring.

The next over was a maiden from Walsh to Atherton, followed by another maiden from Ambrose to Trescothick. Just as it appeared that Walsh's next over to Atherton would bring the third maiden out of four, Walsh produced a delivery which came sharply back in to Atherton, rose equally sharply, and took the shoulder of the bat, giving Campbell a diving catch at second slip; West Indies had the start they desired.

Walsh and Jacobs appeal for a catch off Hussain – but it's not out

Atherton c Campbell b Walsh 1
Trescothick n.o. 0 England 1 - 1

There followed another six overs of frighteningly accurate and aggressive bowling from Ambrose and Walsh, during which Trescothick and Hussain only added two runs, one of which was a leg-bye; Trescothick had not yet scored his first run in test cricket.

Then Adams decided to rest Ambrose, presumably with a view to being able always to have one or the other of his two main bowlers in operation rather than have two weaker bowlers bowling in tandem, but the result was a tremendous and immediate easing of pressure, as Trescothick got off the mark by driving Rose's first delivery, a no-ball, through mid-on for three.

Hussain then launched a tremendous shot at Rose's second ball, hoisting a short delivery high towards the long-leg boundary, where Courtney Walsh took the catch only to take a step backwards as he did so,

Ridley Jacobs and Brian Lara

inadvertently carrying the ball over the boundary and giving six runs to the batsman instead of sending him on his way. A few seconds before the ball came his way Walsh had been chatting on the boundary to the twelfth man who had brought him a bottle of water; whether this had disturbed his concentration it is difficult to say, but there was something ironic in seeing such a player – so miserly with runs that he had not yet conceded any in his first five overs and so accustomed to taking wickets himself – make such an error.

The result of this was that in Rose's first over England's score had advanced by ten, and so far only one legitimate ball had been bowled; in fact a further three runs were to be added before the over was completed. At the other end, however, Walsh then bowled another maiden.

A famous West Indian watches the proceedings – Sir Vivian Richards

Rose's next over was also full of incident, as Trescothick first of all pulled a short ball into the hands of Hinds backward of square, Hinds being however unable to hold on to the catch, and then flashing at a ball outside the off stump and being lucky not to get an edge.

But there was even more incident in Walsh's next over. As had been the case with Atherton, Hussain was trapped by a ball which rose sharply and hit the shoulder of his bat, and this time it was Adams in the gully who took the catch.

Hussain c Adams b Walsh 10
Trescothick n.o. 3 England 17 - 2

Walsh chatting to the twelfth man – was his attention distracted?

The next ball was quite extraordinary. Possibly Graham Thorpe was expecting to be greeted with a bouncer on his return to test cricket, but Walsh bowled a slower ball, a yorker, which Thorpe seemed convinced was going to be a beamer. Whatever his thoughts may have been, he missed the ball completely and was hit on the boot, his walk back to the pavilion being made all the more embarrassing by the laughter of the crowd as they watchd the replay on the giant screen.

Thorpe lbw b Walsh 0
Trescothick n.o. 3 England 17 - 3

This was as good a start as West Indies could have hoped for – although they would have dearly loved Courtney Walsh to take a hat-trick, especially since the next man in was Alec Stewart, batting in his one hundredth test. That was not to be, however, as

Stewart defended his first ball coolly and calmly. At this stage Walsh had taken three wickets for no runs, having bowled seven consecutive maidens.

Seven runs came from Rose's next over, including a classic off drive for four by Trescothick, who then, to Courtney Walsh's disgust, edged the first ball of his next over through the slips to the third man boundary; these were the first runs to be taken from Walsh in the course of eight overs.

Up until the tea interval Stewart and Trescothick were content to take runs from the less menacing bowling of Rose whilst simply playing out those bowled by Walsh – who during that time bowled eleven overs, nine of which were maidens. Rose, by way of contrast, had conceded 33 runs in six overs. Admittedly he could have taken two wickets if catches had been held, but in all truth those would not have

Thorpe deceived first ball by Walsh's yorker

resulted from good bowling, and he was not providing the sort of support Walsh needed, nor was he bowling in accordance with his captain's instructions.

Tea: England 47 - 3
Trescothick n.o. 24 Stewart n.o. 8

After tea a double bowling change took place, King taking over from Rose and Ambrose from Walsh, but two firmly struck boundaries on the off side in King's first over gave notice of Stewart's intentions, which were confirmed, with a maiden from Ambrose intervening, by two more similar shots off the first two balls of the next: sixteen runs had been added to the score in fourteen balls since tea. What is more two further boundaries came in the next over from Ambrose, although these were rather more fortuitous, one coming from the outside edge and the second from the inside edge of Stewart's bat.

Alec Stewart on the way to the nets before the start of play

a different part of the boundary each time.

After eight overs had been bowled since tea and England's score had increased by 43 runs, Adams decided it was time he had a go himself, coming on in place of King, and he immediately bowled a maiden. But Ambrose's next over went for ten, so England's high scoring rate was still maintained. After another thrifty over from Adams, Rose replaced Ambrose, but although he bowled rather better than in his first spell he could not reduce the scoring rate, and in one over Stewart hit him three times to the off side boundary, to

Adams, it has to be said, had been bowling fairly tidily, and had not given much away – in fact he only conceded sixteen runs from his first seven overs, but he never really looked like getting a wicket, and it all looked very much like a holding operation, while waiting for Ambrose and Walsh to be sufficiently rested to come back and bowl again.

Trescothick reached his half-century with a magnificent pull over the square leg boundary for six off Adams, and in the following over the England total surpassed that of the West Indies first innings. Stewart by this time was 82 not out. Shortly after, Adams decided to bring back Walsh and Ambrose to try and achieve a breakthrough before the close of play, but by this time both batsmen were very well set, and all they were able to do was slow down the scoring rate a little, and just over three overs before the close of play, Alec Stewart reached his century off only 136 balls, becoming only the fourth player in cricket history to score a hundred in his hundredth test. By the close of play Trescothick and Stewart were still together, and England had stretched their lead to 39 runs.

Close of play: England 196 - 3
Trescothick n.o. 65
Stewart n.o. 105

Alec Stewart celebrating scoring a century in his 100th test

Alec Stewart gets a standing ovation as he reaches his century

The Third Day

England would be feeling confident about their position at the beginning of the third day, and would expect to make good progress from there, whilst being aware that the first hour, with Ambrose and Walsh fresh, might well be a little difficult, and they would need to take great care during that time; even though Stewart and Trescothick had been in very good form the previous evening, they would have to start afresh today. For the West Indies it was absolutely imperative that they make a quick breakthrough; if they could get rid of both Trescothick and Stewart they would be aware that no one else in the English innings had yet made any runs to speak of. But Adams would also be aware that he could not afford to bowl Ambrose and Walsh for too long at the start of play, because there would be a new ball coming in just over twenty overs time, and he would need to have both of them available for that – unless, that is, Rose and King bowled a good deal better than they had so far, and in any case he would need to give them a bowl early on in order to find out.

Ambrose got the West Indies off to a well nigh perfect start, bowling a leg-cutter which Alec Stewart followed with his bat without moving his feet, and the faintest of edges carried through to the wicket keeper.

Stewart c Jacobs b Ambrose 105
Trescothick n.o. 65 England 196 - 4

Vaughan replaced Stewart, and now life was very difficult for the batsmen. Michael Vaughan had some narrow escapes, as did Marcus Trescothick in the early overs. Survival was now the order of the day, with run-scoring not a priority at present. In fact only two runs had been added in thirty balls; but then the unthinkable (from an English point of view) happened, when Walsh brought a ball back in to Trescothick which struck the knee roll of his back pad before being deflected on to the stumps.

Trescothick b Walsh 66
Vaughan n.o. 1 England 198 - 5

So West Indies were now back in the game, the two English run-scorers being back in the pavilion for the addition of only two runs in the course of just over five overs. The responsibility which now fell upon the shoulders of the two Yorkshiremen Vaughan and White was now tremendous. True, England had a lead, but at present it was only a lead of 41, and if either of them were out it could herald a complete collapse and leave them with a lead of perhaps only 50 or 60, which, given the start they had had, and considering that England would be batting last on a wearing wicket, might very well be inadequate.

They began reasonably confidently, and started to pick up runs here and there. Walsh and Ambrose were obliged to adjust their length with Vaughan and White batting because

Walsh to Trescothick

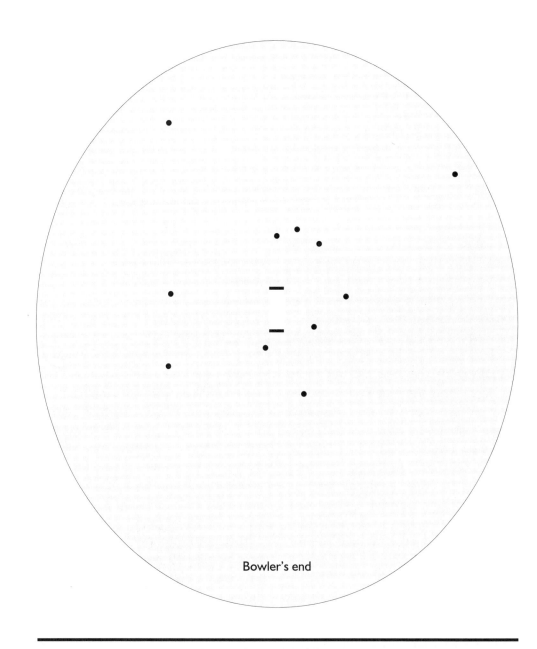

Bowler's end

Walsh's field for Trescothick (right-arm fast, left-hand bat)

Trescothick 66 not out

England 198 - 4

both of them like to play off the front foot, whereas Alec Stewart and Marcus Trescothick both tend to play off the back foot – in fact both of them were trapped in the crease by the balls which dismissed them in this innings. So Ambrose and Walsh now bowled a little shorter, which gave the impression that the wicket was playing a little faster today, although the 'speed gun' which measures the velocity of each delivery did not confirm that impression.

Ten overs into the day Jimmy Adams decided to bring on Rose instead of Ambrose; no doubt to his relief (and to most other people's surprise), Rose's first over was a maiden, as was Walsh's next over.

A further reasonably accurate over from Rose yielded only two runs, and then Walsh was replaced by Reon King, whose bowling had been generally wayward so far throughout the series. His first three deliveries were wide, one almost wide enough to be declared a wide, but his fourth, much faster, was not only on a better line but came in a little and beat Craig White, removing his off bail.

White b King 6

Vaughan n.o. 6 England 210 - 6

Off the next 28 balls only nine runs were added, and only two of those were off the bat, as Vaughan and Cork tried to settle in to their task. Both batsman had narrow escapes, Vaughan nearly playing a ball from Rose off an inside edge onto his stumps and another edge from Cork only prevented from reaching the stumps by the intervention of his body. Then at last Cork unleashed a back foot square drive to the cover boundary, and 28 runs came in the next four overs, England's score advancing to 247 for 6, their lead now being 90. There were only two boundaries in those 28 runs: most of them came as a result of positive running. Cork and

Test Match Special's Christopher Martin-Jenkins taking time off from the commentary box

White realised that very soon Walsh and Ambrose would be at them with the new ball, and they needed to get as many runs as they could in the meantime.

Curtly Ambrose took the new ball at the earliest possible moment, and began his new spell with a maiden to Vaughan. Surprisingly King continued to bowl, and in his first over with the new ball he came close to having Cork caught behind, and also hit Vaughan in the midriff with a really fast, vicious ball; at last Ambrose seemed to be getting some proper support from someone other than Courtney Walsh.

Two singles came early in Ambrose's next over, bringing England's score past the 250 mark, but then Cork wafted his bat at a ball passing just outside off and was caught by Jacobs.

Cork b Jacobs b Ambrose 16
Vaughan n.o. 21 England 251 - 7

Croft and Vaughan then played out the remaining fourteen balls before lunch.

Lunch: England 253 - 7
Vaughan n.o. 23 Croft n.o. 0

England now had a lead of 96, which they would regard as a reasonably comfortable cushion, although they would be disappointed if they did not add at least thirty more runs before their innings ended. West Indies would feel they were now almost there: the new ball was still only five overs old, and Walsh and Ambrose would be coming back after a good rest.

With the third ball after lunch Walsh came very close to dismissing Vaughan with a ball which missed the off stump by the proverbial coat of varnish, but the tension was relieved in Ambrose's next over as three singles, a no-ball and a square drive off the back foot by Croft added eight to the total, all very valuable runs. In the next over Walsh once more thought he had dismissed Vaughan with a perfect slow yorker, but to most people's astonishment, umpire Willey turned down his appeal.

Reon King going back to his mark

But Vaughan was not destined to last much longer, and two overs later he gave an easy slip catch to Brian Lara off the bowling of Ambrose.

Vaughan c Lara b Ambrose 29
Croft n.o. 15 England 275 - 8

Croft and Caddick now seemed determined to add as many as possible to the score, Caddick playing a good shot off his legs to long on for three off the bowling of Walsh, and Croft hitting the next ball, a slow yorker which was over-pitched, to the mid-wicket boundary. Very soon, however, a straight ball from Ambrose which kept a little low sent Caddick on his way, to be replaced by England's last man, Darren Gough.

Caddick lbw b Ambrose 3
Croft n.o. 20 England 283 - 9

Croft did his best to farm the bowling, taking two off Ambrose when three runs would have been possible, and then a single from the last ball of the over, but it was hardly necessary, as Gough, after a cross-batted slog for three off Walsh, hit King for a four and a three off consecutive balls. King's next ball, a no-ball, took England's score to 300. It was King, however, who had the last word where Gough was concerned, although it was mistiming of a an attempted hook by Gough rather than good bowling which brought about the dismissal. The ball rocketed up towards Ambrose at third man, and the England innings was finally over, their lead having increased to a very healthy 146.

Gough c Ambrose b King 12
Croft n.o. 27 England 303 all out

The West Indies now had thirteen overs to face before tea, and uppermost in their mind would be the importance of not losing a wicket during that session. The English bowlers would be feeling fairly confident with a 146 run lead on first innings and the prospect of having only thirteen overs to bowl before being able to have another short rest.

Gough and Caddick opened the bowling, with Campbell and Griffith at the crease for West Indies. There was to be no early wicket for the English bowlers this time, but few easy runs for the batsmen either; after five overs the score was 18 - 0, but half of those had come off the edge.

Former test umpire Dicky Bird

Cork then replaced Andy Caddick, and only one run was scored from each of the next three overs. Then spin was introduced for the first time, with Gough giving way to Robert Croft, who immediately looked to have had Adrian Griffith caught off bat and pad, but the batsman received the benefit of the considerable doubt and Croft was disappointed – although it was equally difficult to make a judgement after seeing several television replays.

In the following over Dominic Cork demonstrated the folly of bowling short and wide outside the off stump, and paid the price by being dispatched twice to the point boundary by Campbell. A further tight over from Croft preceded the tea interval.

Tea: West Indies 35 - 0
Campbell n.o. 21 Griffith n.o. 12

So far neither batsman appeared to be unduly troubled, and the West Indies would now be hoping that this sound start would be consolidated. The English bowlers on the other hand needed to concentrate on line and length, forcing the batsmen to play at every ball.

Cork and Caddick resumed the attack, and the final session of the day began with three maiden overs. A boundary in the next over relieved Campbell's frustration somewhat, but apart from that, only one further run was scored in the first six overs after tea.

Then Croft was brought back into the attack, and for a while it looked as if he was turning the ball sufficiently to cause problems for the batsmen. It was Caddick, however, who nearly got the break-through when an appeal for a catch behind the wicket was

Gough measures his run-up, whilst Cork chats with Hussain

turned down, although television replays suggested the ball had come off Campbell's glove.

After 24 overs the West Indian score had advanced to 51, and Gough returned, only to concede eight runs from his first over to Campbell. Griffith and Campbell then began to exploit the left-hand / right-hand combination by taking quick singles and rotating the strike, in the hope that the bowlers' line would be affected. But life at the crease was not easy, and both batsmen nearly succumbed to yorkers, one from Gough which hit Campbell on the foot and one from Croft which made Griffith fall over. In addition the English fielding was still keen, led by Nasser Hussain who nearly ran out Griffith with a diving shy at the stumps.

But still there was no success for England, and after a four-over spell Gough was replaced by White; two overs later Cork took over from Croft. White and Cork took a couple of overs to get loose, but then Cork produced a fine ball which rose sharply off a length to be taken above his head by Stewart, and Craig White, bowling to a packed leg-side field, speared a ball into Campbell's body. The West Indian opener survived that, but not the next delivery, which was very similar: the ball flew high off his bat out to point, where Cork took the catch.

Campbell c Cork b White 55
Griffith n.o. 31 West Indies 96 - 1

With only about ten overs to go before the close the West Indies would have been disappointed, but with the score on 96 for 1 and the deficit now reduced to 50 they now had much more cause for optimism. But they would be aware that if another wicket were to fall before the close, much of the good work done by the openers would be undone. Moreover the light was deteriorating, and Hinds was struck on the body by the first ball he received from White, which he simply did not see, and the next two or three overs saw the batsmen struggling against the aggression of Cork and White.

At this stage the batsmen would probably have accepted an invitation to leave the field for bad light, but no such invitation came, and it became even less likely to come when Hinds hit three boundaries in quick succession, followed by two more when Gough was reintroduced into the attack.

Former England captain, now radio commentator, Graham Gooch

After that short flurry, however, the final three overs were bowled by Croft and – surprisingly – Trescothick, whose solitary over would have been a maiden had it not been for two wides. (In truth he was rather lucky not to have been called more than twice for bowling wide.)

The day therefore ended rather tamely, with the sides almost on level terms, the West Indies now being only fifteen runs short of the England total.

Close of play: West Indies 131 - 1 Griffith n.o. 41 Hinds n.o. 20

The Fourth Day

The match had now become, to all intents and purposes, a single-innings match. The scores were virtually level, and West Indies had only lost one wicket so far. The basic question for Jimmy Adams was whether or not he wanted to try and win or whether he was content to settle for a draw. But it would be unusual for any West Indian captain to settle for a draw with two days still to go. Jimmy Adams would also be aware that if his side did not bat for the whole day, then they stood a good chance of losing the match. That, then, must be the West Indies' first objective. It must necessarily therefore be England's to try and dismiss them before the end of the day, and preferably before tea.

When play began on the fourth morning, rain was in the air, and in fact it was drizzling as Darren Gough bowled his first ball, a no-ball to Griffith. After that inauspicious start Gough comprehensively beat Griffith three times without conceding a further run.

Craig White, who had been the fastest bowler in the match so far, then came on to begin a new spell, but was only able to bowl five balls before the players had to leave the field because of rain. Fortunately the interruption lasted only four minutes, and when play resumed White completed his over, a maiden, with a ball which struck Hinds on the visor.

Another television commentator – former England captain David Gower

It looked as if the run famine was coming to an end in the next over when Griffith played a fine leg glance to the boundary off Gough, having taken two runs from a similar shot earlier in the over, but then only three runs came from the next 21 balls. Hinds, clearly frustrated at being tied down, then drove Gough to the point boundary, but, trying to repeat the shot off the next ball he only succeeded in edging the ball to Stewart.

Hinds c Stewart b Gough 25
Griffith n.o. 49 West Indies 145 - 2

This constituted an excellent start for England, and a potentially disastrous one for the West Indies, who were still one run short of the England total, and everything now seemed to depend on Brian Lara.

Dominic Cork, who now replaced White, then bowled a maiden to Griffith, and the tension noticeably rose as Gough prepared to bowl to Lara. So far in this series Gough was well ahead on points in their personal battle, but this time Lara was clearly determined to get on top straight away. Having mistimed a pull off the first ball he received, but from which he nevertheless scored two, he then cut the second ball to the point boundary. By the end of the over the West Indies score had advanced by nine runs, which meant they were eight runs ahead of England, and Lara already had seven. Gough was immediately taken out of the attack, to be replaced by White.

Griffith did not mean to be left out, and he brought up his half-century by driving Cork through the covers for four. But then the English bowlers tightened things up a little, and four

Craig White in full flight, bowling to Ramnaresh Sarwan

more overs passed with only five runs being added. At this point Nasser Hussain, always busy and always looking for new lines of attack, brought Croft on to bowl. After four dot-balls, and a fifth delivery from which Lara scored one run to mid-on off the inside edge, Croft then deceived Griffith with a ball which pitched in line and then straightened, and the West Indies were effectively 18 for 3.

Griffith lbw b Croft 54
Lara n.o. 13 West Indies 164 - 3

Jimmy Adams's policy now was to play an anchor role himself, making sure that he did not get out whilst allowing Lara to attack the bowling. The balance then started to swing gradually back towards the West Indies. White and Croft continued for a while, and then Caddick relieved White, with Vaughan taking over from Caddick for the last over before lunch.

The nearest England came to taking Lara's wicket was when a ball from Croft came off bat and pad and went straight through the hands of Cork at silly point; Lara celebrated his lucky escape by hitting Croft straight back over his head for six. It was an unfortunate miss for England, because the West Indian lead at that time was only 45, and with Lara out, England would again have been in control.

The scoring rate between the fall of Griffith's wicket and lunch did not appear to be especially high; in fact 47 runs came in 15 overs. But Lara's personal scoring rate was much higher – virtually a run a ball, whereas Adams had only scored seven while facing 53 balls. The way Lara had overcome his early nervousness and had ridden his luck looked ominous for England.

Lunch: West Indies 211 - 3
Lara n.o. 49 Adams n.o. 7

It was now clearly essential for England to try to get Lara out without further delay, for if he maintained his current strike rate the West Indies could put themselves in a strong enough position to win. After all, if England could turn a match round as they had done at Lord's, it was equally possible for the West Indies, with Walsh and Ambrose, to do the same.

What was perhaps even more ominous was that Lara spent some of the lunch interval in the nets facing a new ball; in the match itself the new ball was due in three overs time. But it was Croft who opened the afternoon session, and who saw his first ball pulled over mid-wicket to bring up Lara's fifty; then, in Croft's final over before Gough took the new ball, Lara played a majestic cover drive for another four.

The new ball made little difference. In Caddick's first two overs Lara found the boundary three times. Two overs later it was Gough's turn to be punished, with eleven runs conceded in the over, ten of them to Lara and one no-ball.

With the new ball bowlers having no success, Nasser Hussain turned once more to the spin of Croft, but Adams edged the first ball of his new spell through the slips for three to bring up the century partnership and give the West Indies a lead of 120. What was more, runs were now coming thick and fast – 40 runs in the last seven overs – and something needed to be done.

Hussain's policy was to try and close down one end by bowling Croft, even though the ball was still pretty new, and persevering with Caddick, who was bowling very well but without much luck, at the other end. During this period of play there was certainly enough happening to keep the bowlers and the fielders interested, as both batsmen played and missed, dug out yorkers and dodged rising fast balls, but the runs kept coming, and by the time drinks were taken half way through the afternoon, the score had risen to 277 for 3, 66 having been scored in 15 overs since lunch. Lara's share of the total was now 96.

The answer could well be to try to frustrate Lara and force him into playing rash shots by restricting his scoring opportunities, and this is what Nasser Hussain tried to do after the break by bringing on Cork at one end and persevering with Croft at the other. Cork succeeded in preventing Lara from scoring off the first three balls of his over, although two of them were hit very hard, each going straight to a fielder. But the fourth ball sped like a rocket through the covers, and Lara had reached three figures for the first time in the series.

At the other end Adams seemed to be intent on not scoring, even refusing to play an aggressive shot when Croft tossed the ball up to him. It was a tactic that could conceivably misfire, however: if England's current strategy

Gough appeals unsuccessfully for lbw against Jimmy Adams

was to slow down the scoring rate, this could only play into their hands.

The sharpness of the English fielding coupled with some accurate bowling at least had the required effect of stemming the flow of runs, with only four runs coming from the next six overs, but still no wicket fell in that time. There were signs of Lara becoming frustrated, which is what England were hoping for. He launched a huge drive at Cork and just missed getting an edge; he played a massive sweep to a ball from Croft, and missed completely, and then when he did make contact with a similar shot, the ball went up in the air in the direction of mid-wicket, and he only scored two runs. In other words, the free-scoring Lara of a few overs before appeared to have been replaced by the uncertain Lara of the earlier games in the series.

At last Lara made proper contact once more, and hit Croft to the mid-wicket boundary, which was the signal for another bowling change, with Craig White coming into the attack instead of Cork. White's first ball to Adams was edged towards Trescothick at slip, but did not quite carry; his second was also edged, and Trescothick might even have got his fingers to it if he had chosen to dive. The remaining balls of the over were equally testing, but when the end of the over came Adams was still there, although no more runs had been scored.

Croft was then replaced by Vaughan, with an ultra-defensive field, but Lara did not seem to want to take the singles which were clearly on offer, and the only runs that came in that over were four byes from a wayward delivery which beat both Lara and Stewart to bring up the West Indian 300.

Adams then played the first ball of White's next over to Hussain at short mid-wicket. Hussain noticed that Lara was backing up a long way and shied at the stumps: a direct hit meant that at last England had the wicket for which they had been striving so hard, and Lara was on his way back to the pavilion.

Lara run out 112
Adams n.o. 27 West Indies 302 - 4

Another one flies to the boundary

Vaughan to Lara

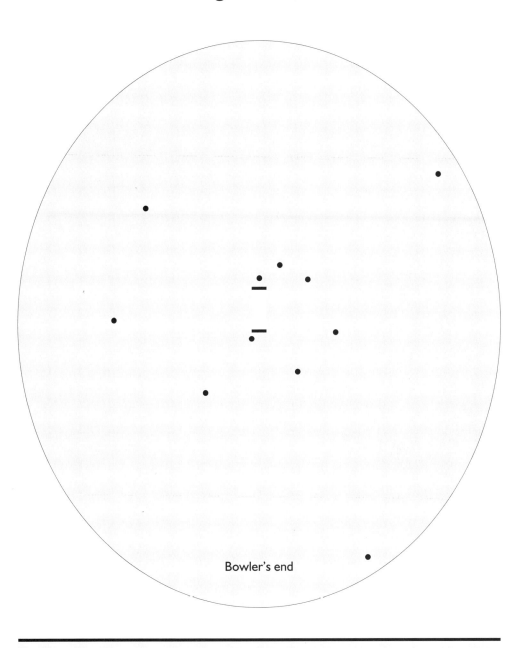

Bowler's end

Vaughan's field for Lara (right-arm off-spin, left-hand bat)

Lara 112 not out

West Indies 298 - 3

Adams was now joined by Sarwan, and together they safely negotiated the remainder of White's over and a further over from Croft, the last before the tea interval. Nasser Hussain's object in bringing Croft back so soon was obviously to pressurise the new batsman, but the strategy did not work because they allowed Sarwan to take a single off the first ball he received, and Adams played out the rest of the over.

**Tea interval: West Indies 305 - 4
Adams n.o. 29 Sarwan n.o. 1**

Sarwan uses a bail to mark his ground

The West Indian lead of 159 with only four wickets down was enough to make them feel reasonably optimistic with regard to the final outcome, but still not enough to feel totally secure, and they needed to make sure that they batted until the close of play, preferably without losing any more wickets. In some ways the number of runs they scored was immaterial, because if they scored so many that England were set a target beyond their reach, the English batsmen would be unlikely to take risks and therefore be less likely to get out.

Certainly Sarwan and Adams did not seem to be in a hurry to score runs off White and Croft, and only six runs came from the first four overs after tea, but then three confident shots from Sarwan which brought him eight runs, followed by a sweep to the leg-side boundary by Adams off Croft suddenly brought the game to life again.

But not for long. Caddick now came into the attack, and not only did the scoring rate slow down again but he bowled with such aggression that Sarwan in particular had a very torrid time, with the ball constantly rising into his ribs from just short of a length and at speeds up to 86 mph. In the meantime Croft, bowling from the Warwick Road end as he had done almost throughout the innings, kept things fairly tight apart from one ball which drifted down the leg side and which Adams put away fine for four.

Considering the way Caddick had been attacking Sarwan it was no surprise when, in the fourth over of his new spell, after fending off yet another rising ball, Sarwan was deceived by a ball of fuller length, and umpire Cowie had no hesitation in giving him out leg before.

**Sarwan lbw b Caddick 19
Adams n.o. 41 West Indies 335 - 5**

Caddick greeted the West Indian wicket-keeper with a short ball which he took on the chest, but after surviving a stumping attempt by Stewart off Croft and a missed catch in the slips by Trescothick, Jacobs started to play with more confidence, and the West Indian lead soon passed 200.

Cork then replaced Croft and Gough took over from Caddick, although Cork's new spell was interrupted after only one over by a further over from Croft off which Ridley Jacobs hit two fours and was lucky not to be given out lbw. Cork then continued until the close of play, with White returning to replace Gough to bowl the last two overs of the day from the Stretford end.

During this period scoring remained fairly slow, although Ridley Jacobs hit Cork for four over mid-on and Jimmy Adams also hit Cork to the boundary to bring up his half-century, which had taken 282 minutes, during which time he had faced 214 balls. It was a typically dour but crucial innings from Adams. Dominic Cork soon had his revenge, however, for with his very next ball (in fact the first ball of his next over), he at last dismissed the West Indian captain, trapping him leg before.

Adams lbw b Cork 53
Jacobs n.o. 25 West Indies 373 - 6

Franklyn Rose then came to join Ridley Jacobs, and hit the second ball he received for four, but after that the West Indian batsmen were content to play out the remaining two overs, and so the penultimate day's play ended with the West Indians 235 in front: a good day's work for them, considering they had been so far behind on first innings.

Close of play: West Indies 381 - 6
Jacobs n.o. 25 Rose n.o. 8

Cork bowling to Sarwan

The Fifth Day

At the start of the final day's play Jimmy Adams had a number of options open to him:

♦ Declare immediately, giving England 90 overs to score 236 or alternatively give his bowlers the opportunity to get England out for less than 235 within 90 overs;
♦ Bat for another hour, scoring as quickly as possible, taking the score to perhaps 450, giving England 305 to make in 75 overs;
♦ Bat until lunch, when the score would possibly be about 480, giving England 335 to get in 60 overs;
♦ Simply bat on, with no thought of declaring, but making as many runs as possible.

It had been clear on the fourth day that the wicket was fairly slow and was not giving much assistance to the bowlers. To give England a target as low as 236 in a day would almost guarantee defeat for the West Indies, and was not a genuine option.

The fourth option was probably not realistic either, as that would probably ensure that the game would end in a draw, and Adams would feel at this stage that he had a genuine chance of winning.

The question for Adams was how long his bowlers would need if they were to bowl England out. It would depend to a certain extent on whether England were trying to win or not; if they did not have a reachable target to aim at they would simply go into defensive mode, and the chances of the West Indies winning would recede. Sixty overs could well be enough, but Adams would have to bear in mind that Walsh and Ambrose could only bowl half of those overs between them, and would need better support from their colleagues than they had had in the first innings.

A declaration was therefore the most likely scenario (unless, of course, England took the remaining four wickets quickly), but the timing would depend on the progress made by the remaining batsmen. The second option, involving another hour's batting, would seem to be where the smart money would go.

White and Cork opened the day's proceedings, but there was no indication to begin with that West Indies were out for quick runs and an early declaration, as the first fifteen balls only yielded three runs. Then off the fourth ball of White's second over Rose walked across his stumps, as he had done many times before; this time the ball hit his back leg, and umpire Cowie had no hesitation in giving him out.

Rose lbw b White 10
Jacobs n.o. 26 West Indies 384 - 7

This was certainly not what West Indies would have wanted, but Jacobs and Ambrose now tried to increase the scoring rate. However, apart from a lofted drive over mid-on by Jacobs in Cork's second over they had difficulty finding the boundary.

Eight overs into the day's play Croft relieved Cork, and a cover drive for two by Ambrose brought up the West Indian 400. Two overs later Ambrose at last made proper contact and lofted the ball high over Croft's head and into the stand, but apart from that, his efforts to hit the ball very hard were largely unsuccessful, although he and Jacobs did at least keep the scoreboard ticking over.

Then Cork returned and was immediately swung over mid-wicket for four by Ambrose; in all nine runs came from that over, eight of them to Ambrose, who proceeded to take eight more from White's next over. It looked as if the anticipated run-chase had at last arrived, but then Nasser Hussain brought back Gough and Croft, and only eight runs came from the next four overs.

At that point Jimmy Adams decided he had enough runs in the bank and declared the innings closed, leaving England 293 to win in 79 overs.

Innings declared closed:
West Indies 438 - 7
Jacobs n.o. 42 Ambrose n.o. 36

Darren Gough in action

In one-day match terms an asking rate of 293 in 79 overs would be fairly reasonable, but in a test match, with no fielding restrictions and less stringent application of the laws governing wides, it would represent a great achievement if England were to win this match. It was not, however, altogether out of the question, and much would depend on the early overs. One thing in England's favour would be that, with less than eighty overs to be bowled, the West Indies would not have the benefit of a second new ball later in the day. But the England openers would have no thought of winning at this stage; they would merely be thinking of keeping their wickets intact until lunch and taking whatever runs were on offer. If, at a later stage in the day, the target appeared to be achievable, only then would a plan be put in place to ensure a victory.

Ambrose and Walsh began in their usual hostile fashion, but neither Atherton nor Trescothick was unduly troubled, although Trescothick's first boundary did come from an edge through the slips. Shortly afterwards though, he hit first Ambrose and then Walsh to the leg-side boundary. Atherton played more circumspectly: it was not until King replaced Walsh that Atherton hit his first boundary, a majestic square drive.

By the time lunch arrived England had achieved their objective of not losing a wicket, and looked fairly secure. They still needed 251 from the remaining two sessions, which looked unlikely, but not impossible.

Lunch interval: England 42 - 0
Atherton n.o. 15
Trescothick n.o. 26

When only two runs came from the first five overs after lunch an England win looked even more unlikely. When the players were then obliged to leave the field because of rain it seemed more improbable still, especially when the interruption lasted for 52 minutes.

**Rain stopped play: England 44 - 0
Atherton n.o. 16
Trescothick n.o. 26**

On the resumption Ambrose and Walsh continued – having been able to profit from an unscheduled rest period – but now the scoring rate increased, with 17 runs coming from four overs. But then off the first ball of the fifth over after the rain-break Walsh had Atherton caught behind by Jacobs.

**Atherton c Jacobs b Walsh 28
Trescothick n.o. 30 England 61 - 1**

Only three overs later the players had to leave the field once more for rain.

**Rain stopped play: England 63 - 1
Trescothick n.o. 31 Hussain n.o. 1**

This time the interruption lasted for 79 minutes – although tea was taken during this period to reduce the amount of actual playing time lost – and it was clear by the time the players returned that no result was now possible. In fact a further nine overs were then bowled, during which time Trescothick and Nasser Hussain took the score to 80 for 1, but after four balls of the next over, at 5.20 pm, the umpires decided the light was poor

Another celebration, but too late this time

and the two captains agreed that there was no point in continuing.

So a game which had swung first one way and then the other ended in anti-climax, a potentially thrilling last day ruined by bad weather.

**Close of play: England 80 - 1
Trescothick n.o. 38 Hussain n.o. 6
Match drawn**

Jimmy Adams was probably disappointed that rain had robbed him of a possible victory after his side had staged an impressive fight-back following his ill-judged decision to bat first. Nasser Hussain was probably also disappointed that he had allowed the West Indies to recover from an apparently losing position at the end of the second day, but both captains would also be feeling relieved that they had not lost, and the series remained tied at one game all with two matches still to play.

Match Scorecard

West Indies	First Innings		Second Innings	
Campbell	c Thorpe b Gough	2	c Cork b White	55
Griffith	lbw b Caddick	2	lbw b Croft	54
Hinds	c Stewart b Cork	26	c Stewart b Gough	25
Lara	c Thorpe b Gough	13	run out	112
Adams	c Thorpe b White	22	lbw b Cork	53
Sarwan	lbw b Cork	36	lbw b Caddick	19
Jacobs	b Caddick	7	not out	42
Rose	lbw b Cork	16	lbw b White	10
Ambrose	c Hussain b Caddick	3	not out	36
King	not out	3	(Did not bat)	
Walsh	lbw b Cork	7	(Did not bat)	
Extras	b1, lb8, w2, nb 6	20	b14, lb4, w2, nb12	32
Total	(71.1 overs, 314 min)	157	(165 overs, 623 min)	438 - 7 dec.

Fall of wickets:
First innings: 1-3, 2-12, 3-49, 4-49, 5-118, 6-126, 7-130, 8-135, 9-148
Second innings: 1-96, 2-145, 3-164, 4-302, 5-335, 6-373, 7-384
Bowling:
Gough 21-3-58-2, Caddick 24-10-45-3
Cork 17.1-8-23-4, White 9-1-18-1

Gough 27-5-96-1, Caddick 23-4-64-1
Cork 28-9-64-1, Croft 47-8-124-1
Trescothick 1-0-2-0, Vaughan 2-1-3-0

England	First Innings		Second Innings	
Atherton	c Campbell b Walsh	1	c Jacobs b Walsh	28
Trescothick	c Lara b Ambrose	66	not out	38
Hussain	c Adams b Walsh	10	not out	6
Thorpe	lbw b Walsh	0	(Did not bat)	
Stewart	c Jacobs b Ambrose	105	(Did not bat)	
Vaughan	c Lara b Ambrose	29	(Did not bat)	
White	b King	6	(Did not bat)	
Cork	c Jacobs b Ambrose	16	(Did not bat)	
Croft	not out	27	(Did not bat)	
Caddick	lbw b Ambrose	3	(Did not bat)	
Gough	c Ambrose b King	12.	(Did not bat)	
Extras	b10, lb6, nb12	28	B3, lb 8, w 1, nb 12	24
Total	(97.2 overs, 424 min)	303	(33.4 overs, 133 min)	80 - 1

Fall of wickets:
First innings: 1-1, 2-17, 3-17, 4-196, 5-198, 6-210, 7-251, 8-275, 9-283
Second innings: 1-61
Bowling:
Ambrose 27-7-70-4, Walsh 27-14-50-4
Rose 20-3-83-0, King 12.2-3-52-2
Adams 11-4-32-0

Ambrose 22-11-22-1, Walsh 23.5-5-74-6
Rose 16-3-67-1, King 8-2-17-0

Match drawn

The Fourth Test

Headingley

The Weather

At the start of the match there was quite a lot of blue sky, but also a lot of cloud. The forecast was for sunny spells and scattered showers, some heavy, and it was expected to be quite windy.

The Pitch

The pitch looked likely to be two-paced: there were some quite grassy parts, but also some very dry patches, and even some cracks. When the ball hit a grassy patch it would be likely to lift, but on hitting a bare patch it would be more likely to skid through. As for the cracks, if there was much sunshine during the match they would be likely to get wider, and balls hitting them would be unpredictable. There also appeared to be a fair degree of moisture under the surface – less than at Edgbaston, but more than at Old Trafford, and the indications were that batting might turn out to be quite difficult, especially in the early stages but also later in the game.

Team Selection

Both teams made one change from Old Trafford, England bringing in Graeme Hick as a seventh specialist batsman and West Indies replacing Rose with Nixon McLean; Rose was suffering from a sprained ankle, but would probably have been omitted anyway because his bowling form had been less than impressive.

England	West Indies
Atherton	Campbell
TrescothicK	Griffith
Hussain (Capt)	Hinds
Thorpe	Lara
Stewart (Wkt)	Adams (Capt)
Vaughan	Sarwan

Hick	Jacobs (Wkt)
White	McLean
Cork	Ambrose
Caddick	King
Gough	Walsh

Umpires: D. Cowie & G. Sharpe

The Toss

West Indies again won the toss, and Jimmy Adams again decided to bat,

Chairman of Selectors David Graveney

despite the experience of Old Trafford where batting first appeared with hindsight to have been the wrong option. His thinking was almost certainly that, although the pitch might be difficult at first, it would get better for a time before deteriorating on the fourth and fifth days. If his batsmen could play out the difficult first session without too many mishaps, then they might have a chance of posting a decent score. Certainly the prospect of batting last on a pitch such as this did not look particularly inviting.

Nasser Hussain said that he too would probably have batted if he had won the toss – and probably for the same reasons – but he was not too unhappy to bowl first.

Immediate Aims

Jimmy Adams would be hoping that his batsmen would be able this time to justify his decision to bat first, and would be desperately hoping that they could reach the lunch interval without losing a wicket. Nasser Hussain would be hoping that his fast bowlers would be able to exploit the favourable conditions, given that batting would probably become easier later in the day; he would certainly be hoping for two, and preferably three wickets before lunch.

The First Day

Darren Gough opened the proceedings, bowling to Sherwin Campbell from the Football Ground end, with a strong breeze blowing from off to leg. As expected, he had a very attacking field, with three slips, two gullies, a backward point, a short mid-wicket, mid-off and fine leg. His first ball was firmly driven to the off side by Campbell, and a misfield by Nasser Hussain yielded two runs. Despite the wind Gough still managed to move the ball away from the right-hander; Caddick too got a great deal of movement, and very nearly dismissed Griffith with his first ball, an in-swinging yorker which Griffith did well to survive.

In Gough's next over Campbell played a perfect drive through the covers for four, but trying to repeat the shot off the next ball he failed to get his foot across, and only succeeded in giving a chest-high catch to Trescothick in the gully.

Darren Gough

Campbell c Trescothick b Gough 8
Griffith n.o. 2 West Indies 11 - 1

Sherwin Campbell

After a maiden from Caddick, Gough once more tried the ploy which had succeeded in his first over; inviting the off-drive, from which Hinds opened his account with a boundary, then inviting a repeat off the next ball. But Hinds declined to go the same way as Campbell; his reward was to be hit painfully on the thigh from a ball with extra bounce. Then in Gough's next over Hinds was lucky to survive as the English fast bowler continued his probing on or just outside off stump, when he edged a ball which fell just short of White in the gully.

During the course of the next four overs only one run was scored, as extravagant swing and uneven bounce made batting difficult. Then, after twelve overs had been bowled and with the score 35 for 1, there was a double bowling change, with White coming on at the Football Ground end and Cork at the Kirkstall Lane end. Within four overs the score had advanced to 50 for 1, and both batsmen looked fairly comfortable, despite Griffith having been hit on the chest by Cork.

But the position was about to change dramatically. The first ball of White's next over was of good length, pitched just outside off and came in, taking the inside edge of Hinds' bat on its way through to the wicket-keeper.

Hinds c Stewart b White 16
Griffith n.o. 22 West Indies 50 - 2

Brian Lara obviously felt in the mood to carry on where he had left off at Old Trafford and thumped his first ball to the mid-wicket boundary for four. Nasser Hussain's response was to bring back Darren Gough, who had already dismissed Lara three times in the series. But Gough did not even get a chance to bowl to Lara this time because, after Griffith had played out a maiden from Gough, White, bowling round the wicket, dismissed Lara with a ball which came in sharply from outside the off stump to which Lara offered no stroke.

Lara lbw b White 4
Griffith n.o. 22 West Indies 54 - 3

Gough continued to bowl, however, still probing outside off stump and tempting Griffith to cut; but Griffith edged the ball to Stewart, and West Indies were now in some disarray.

Griffith c Stewart b Gough 22
Adams n.o. 2 West Indies 56 - 4

But worse was yet to come for the West Indies, who would now have been hoping that Adams and Sarwan would play as effectively as they had done at Old Trafford, but almost immediately Adams dragged an over-pitched delivery from White on

Craig White

to his stumps, and half the West Indian side had now gone, including all the major batsmen apart from the young Sarwan. Craig White had now taken 3 for 13 from less than five overs, and all five wickets had been taken by Yorkshire bowlers on their home ground.

Adams b White 2
Sarwan n.o. 4 West Indies 60 - 5

Much now depended on Sarwan and Jacobs, who needed to bat for a long time if the West Indies were to recover from the hole into which they had dug themselves. Their first aim, however, was to survive until lunch.

Brian Lara and Jimmy Adams

They did survive until lunch, but it was by no means easy. Both batsmen were beaten outside the off stump by out-swingers and were lucky not to get an edge, Jacobs had a narrow escape when the ball hit his glove and just fell short of forward short leg, and then Sarwan appeared to have gloved the ball to Stewart but was given the benefit of the doubt by the umpire. The third umpire was also called into play to adjudicate on a very close run-out attempt, and Jacobs had to receive medical attention when he was hit on the finger by a ball from Gough. But at least they did survive until lunch; what is more, they had added 23 valuable runs in the process.

Lunch interval: West Indies 83 - 5
Sarwan n.o. 22 Jacobs n.o. 5

During the pre-lunch period Sarwan had out-scored Jacobs by 18 runs to 5. After lunch there were really two options. The first was to continue in that way, with Jacobs playing a supporting role and Sarwan taking whatever scoring opportunities arose; Jacobs was also capable of pushing the score along, but his chance would come if Sarwan should chance to get out. The alternative option would be the reverse, with Jacobs taking what runs he could and Sarwan ensuring that he stayed in long enough to give encouragement to the lower order batsmen. Whichever way they did it, one of them needed to play an anchor role, the other needed to score runs.

Ramnaresh Sarwan

mid-off in Cork's first over as he started to go for his shots, but a few minutes later he played a similar shot, and this time Caddick hardly had to move to get to the ball.

Jacobs c Caddick b Cork 35
Sarwan n.o. 35 West Indies 128 - 6

McLean now took Jacobs' place at the crease, and a short passage of play ensued which was very eventful, with the ball whistling past the outside edge, unsuccessful appeals for lbw and one for a catch behind, culminating in McLean getting another outside edge; this time Stewart dived to his left and took a stunning catch right in front of

At first it appeared that they had taken the first of the two options, and after six overs from Caddick and Gough Sarwan was still outscoring Jacobs, but then Caddick over-pitched and Jacobs played a scintillating drive to the long-off boundary. Caddick then over-compensated, and found Jacobs pulling two short balls in succession to the square leg boundary. This meant that 35 runs had been added in seven overs since lunch, and the West Indies score had virtually doubled since the fall of the fifth wicket. One over later a shower of rain took the players off the field; by now the West Indian score was looking almost respectable.

Rain stopped play:
West Indies 119 - 5
Sarwan n.o. 29 Jacobs n.o. 31

Fortunately the break only lasted nine minutes. Cork and White now took over the attack, and Jacobs was lucky not to give a catch to Caddick at

Alec Stewart

White to Sarwan

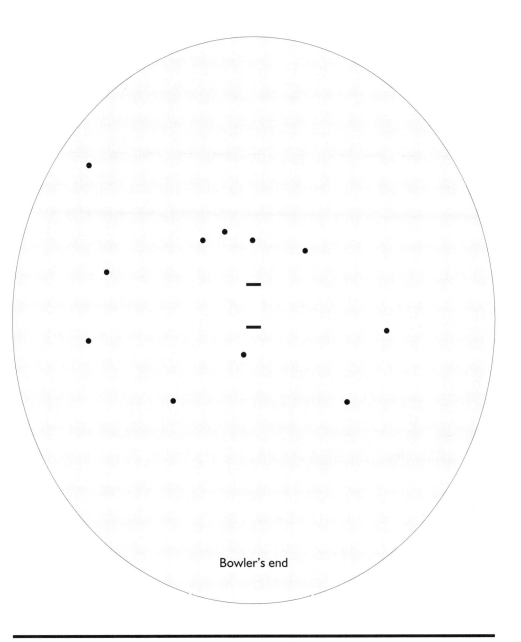

Bowler's end

White's field for Sarwan (right-arm fast-medium, right-hand bat)

Sarwan 35 not out

West Indies 128 - 5

Atherton, who had been expecting to take the catch himself.

McLean c Stewart b White 7
Sarwan n.o. 41 West Indies 143 - 7

Sarwan in the meantime was playing beautifully, but looked as if he would soon run out of partners as Ambrose played a ball from Cork on to his stumps.

Ambrose b Cork 1
Sarwan n.o. 45 West Indies 148 - 8

Reon King took a single off his first ball to give the strike to Sarwan, who then retained the strike by taking another single off the last ball of the over; this was sensible batting. White then bowled a maiden to Sarwan, and Nasser Hussain brought back Gough

Nixon McLean

to try to finish off the West Indian innings. But King again took a single, and Sarwan took three from the last ball to retain the strike once more.

A single from the first ball of White's next over brought Sarwan to a well-deserved 50. King then proceeded to hit White straight for four followed by an easy single, whereupon Sarwan hit two consecutive boundaries, one through the covers and one to square leg. Thus fourteen runs had come off one over from White after he had only conceded 42 from the previous 13 overs.

But then King found himself facing Gough again, and received a delivery which was both too fast and too straight for him; he walked straight into it, and was out leg before.

King lbw b Gough 7
Sarwan n.o. 56 West Indies 168 - 9

Walsh then came to join Sarwan, but the youngster only had time to add two to his score before Walsh chipped another catch to Caddick, this time at mid-wicket.

Walsh c Caddick b White 1
Sarwan n.o. 60
West Indies 172 all out

The break between the innings was combined with the tea interval, which meant that the time lost for rain had been made up without adding to the total day's play.

At this stage both sides would have mixed feelings. Jimmy Adams would be feeling disappointed at his side only making 172 after he had chosen to bat first, particularly since, although the bowling had been good, quite a number of the wickets had fallen because of bad shots. At the same time he would be feeling relieved that they had been able to recover to 172 after having been 60 for 5.

Nasser Hussain, on the other hand, would be feeling disappointed that they had allowed West Indies to recover in this way, but at the start of play he would have been happy if he had known that the West Indies would only make 172 in their first innings.

It was now up to the England batsmen to make sure that they did not make the same kinds of mistake that their opponents had made; they needed if possible to bat not only for the remainder of the first day – and there were 41 overs left in the day – but also for the whole of the second to put themselves into a potentially winning position. The West Indian bowlers would however know that there was something in the pitch for the bowlers, and would feel that if Walsh and Ambrose bowled with their normal accuracy they would get results; the key once more would probably be the extent to which their other bowlers, on this occasion King and McLean, were able to offer adequate support to their main attack.

Trescothick and Atherton

The first ball of the England innings was bowled by Curtly Ambrose, and was steered by Atherton to the third man boundary. Ambrose then retaliated by beating the England opener, first of all just outside the off stump, then again by an off-cutter which passed just over the stumps. Rain was falling as Walsh measured out his run-up – in fact it continued to drizzle for some time – but fortunately it did not rain very hard, and play was not interrupted. Marcus Trescothick's day was soon interrupted though, as Ambrose had him caught at first slip off an out-swinger with extra bounce.

Trescothick c Lara b Ambrose 1
Atherton n.o. 6 England 7 - 1

This was an important breakthrough for the West Indies because Trescothick had been enjoying a very good summer since being brought first into the England one-day squad and then into the test team, and he was brimming with confidence. They would be further encouraged by the fact that his place at the crease was to be taken by Nasser Hussain, who had been having an appalling season with the bat; what was more, Hussain was comprehensively beaten by the first ball he received from Ambrose, but managed to survive.

Brian Lara and Ridley Jacobs

Curtly Ambrose

Walsh then mounted a leg-stump attack on Michael Atherton, trying to tempt him to play into the hands of short leg, but the tactic did not succeed. But in the next over, after Hussain had played two confident shots, one for two runs and one for a single, Ambrose took the outside edge of Atherton's bat, and Lara took another catch at slip. This was the seventeenth time Ambrose had dismissed Atherton, and also Curtly Ambrose's 400th test wicket. It was typical of the spirit in which this series was being played that the West Indian bowler received a standing ovation from the Headingley crowd despite just having made a substantial dent in England's hopes of matching the West Indian total.

**Atherton c Lara b Ambrose 6
Hussain n.o. 3 England 10 - 2**

Hussain and Thorpe then endured eight torrid overs from Walsh and Ambrose, who were moving the ball both ways and achieving greater bounce than had the England bowlers, and by the time King took over from Walsh, only 14 runs had been scored in 13 overs, including the four scored by Atherton off the first ball of the innings. But King's first ball was clipped by Thorpe to the mid-wicket boundary, and immediately the pressure was relieved somewhat.

King's next over was a maiden, but mainly because nearly every ball was wide enough to leave alone, and when Thorpe hit the first ball of a new over from Ambrose for four, this seemed to unsettle the great man, and he proceeded to bowl three no-balls in the over.

King continued to bowl short and wide, but this time Hussain was not content just to watch the ball go by, and he hit two boundaries. King was then joined by McLean, and the runs started to flow more freely; 64 runs had come from 11 overs since Walsh had left the attack, compared with 14 from the first 13 overs. Adams decided enough was enough, and reintroduced Walsh, whilst keeping faith with McLean at the other end.

The result was three maidens out of the next four overs; it would have been four but for an edge from Hussain off Walsh which fell short of second slip and ran away to third man for two. Then in Walsh's next over he bowled a full-length ball which pitched on the stumps, Hussain played outside the ball and was trapped lbw.

Hussain lbw b Walsh 22
Thorpe n.o. 39 England 80 - 3

Another celebration for Courtney Walsh

The partnership between Hussain and Thorpe had been very productive and had put England back in with a chance of matching the West Indian first innings score after having made a disastrous start. Stewart now came to join his Surrey colleague Thorpe, and it was vital from England's point of view that they should not lose another wicket in the remaining twelve overs of the day.

The flow of runs was now stemmed, with only 13 coming from the next six overs. Then Walsh struck once more, trapping Thorpe in front of his stumps with a ball which pitched in line and straightened a little; Walsh had now taken 2 for 11 from 11.4 overs, with 7 maidens.

Thorpe lbw b Walsh 46
Stewart n.o. 3 England 93 - 4

Michael Vaughan came in with only six overs and two balls of the day's play remaining, and he was clearly only interested in survival, not in scoring runs.

Adams persisted with Walsh and McLean, and in Walsh's next over he got the ball to move late away from Alec Stewart as he tried to play it

Michael Vaughan

140

straight, and it went off the outside edge into the hands of Campbell in the slips.

Stewart c Campbell b Walsh 5
Vaughan n.o. 1 England 96 - 5

This was a severe blow for England, since Stewart had been in great form throughout the summer, and it also tipped the balance, probably for the first time, in favour of the West Indies. At least England had another specialist batsman to come in the shape of Graeme Hick, but Hussain decided to keep him back and send in Caddick as a night-watchman.

But judgment on that would have to wait till the next day, as both Vaughan and Caddick were still at the crease when stumps were drawn, and England were trailing by 67 runs.

Close of play: England 105 - 5
Vaughan n.o. 6 Caddick n.o. 3

Whether this was a wise decision on the part of Hussain would remain to be seen. There had already been much discussion in the press about the policy of putting Hick as low as number seven in the batting order, but at least that guaranteed that he would have a specialist batsman to partner when he came in. Promoting Caddick above him meant that Graeme Hick would come in at number eight, and if the next wicket to fall were to be that of Vaughan, then he would only have Caddick, White, Cork and Gough to bat with.

The Second Day

Adams would be feeling that he needed to get the five remaining wickets during the pre-lunch session, because by that time England would undoubtedly be in the lead. England's immediate aim would be for Caddick the night-watchman to stay in as long as possible, and help Vaughan to get near to the West Indian score by the time Hick came to the crease.

As one would expect, Ambrose and Walsh opened the day's proceedings: three runs to Vaughan from Ambrose's opening over, then, almost inevitably, a maiden from Walsh to Vaughan. Caddick then survived a testing over from Ambrose, and the partnership began to flourish, with some good running between the wickets putting the fielders under pressure and earning more runs from overthrows.

Eventually, however, Caddick got an edge to a lifting ball from Ambrose outside off stump, and Jacobs took the catch. Andy Caddick's share of the partnership had only been 6, but they had added 28 to the England score, and the difference was now only 48 runs. What is more, Caddick had survived the first 6½ overs of the day from Ambrose and Walsh, and they would soon need a rest.

Caddick c Jacobs b Ambrose 6
Vaughan n.o. 20 England 124 - 6

At last Hick came to the wicket. He defended the remaining three balls of Ambrose's over, then watched as Vaughan played out a maiden from Walsh. Another over from Ambrose, then King came on to replace Walsh.

Was that a tactical error on Jimmy Adams's part? Walsh had only bowled four overs so far this morning, and it was vital to break this partnership early. But Adams's dilemma was this: if he continued to bowl Ambrose and Walsh in tandem they would both tire at the same time, and he would have to bowl two lesser bowlers together. By rotating them he could at least maintain the pressure at one end, even if the support bowler at the other end was ineffective.

Ridley Jacobs

But Hick did something to relieve the pressure himself when he seized on a short ball from Ambrose and pulled it to the mid-wicket boundary. It was a shot which gave heart not only to the batsman but also to the rest of the England players, to say nothing of their supporters.

Even so, runs came slowly, until Ambrose was obliged to leave the attack after a spell of eight overs. But Adams did not replace him with Walsh as one might have expected. Instead he brought on McLean; Hick smashed his first delivery to the boundary. Suddenly the trickle of runs now became a flood, with 30 coming from four overs, and, after 19 overs of the day's play had gone, the scores were now level, England had only lost six wickets, Hick had 30 and Vaughan 27, and England were once more in the driving seat.

Graeme Hick

four balls produced no runs, but the fifth was cut by Hick for two, and England had reached 200, a lead of 28. One ball later it was lunch-time, and the England batsmen returned to the pavilion rather more cheerfully than most of their predecessors, having succeeded in putting together an as yet unbroken partnership of 76.

It was time for Walsh to return, and immediately Hick found batting more difficult; after surviving a huge lbw appeal he was struck painfully on the hand. The first over of Walsh's new spell was predictably a maiden. But not the second, for Walsh dropped the first ball uncharacteristically short and wide, and Hick cut it hard to the fence. Runs were now starting to come more easily as Hick grew in confidence, and two more cuts to the boundary off McLean helped England's cause considerably.

At last Jimmy Adams decided it was time he had a bowl himself; the first

Lunch interval: England 200 - 6
Vaughan n.o. 37 Hick n.o. 45

It would normally be more or less a reflex action for Jimmy Adams to begin a new session in a situation such as this by bringing on his two strike bowlers Ambrose and Walsh, but on this occasion he continued where he had left off, with McLean at the Football Ground end and himself at the Kirkstall Lane end.

The reason for this was simple: in only eleven overs time the new ball would be due, and he would need Ambrose and Walsh to take it. If they bowled now, they would probably be too tired to use it effectively. Consequently he was viewing the intervening period as one in which they must concentrate on damage limitation, conceding as few runs as possible. It was risky, and illustrates very well the lack of confidence Jimmy Adams had in his support bowlers, but it was none the less a realistic appraisal.

The situation for the West Indies now was better than Adams must have hoped for at lunch; England were only 51 ahead, only Cork and Gough were to come, and the new ball was due in six overs time.

But Vaughan and Cork had made the same calculation, and proceeded to take runs whenever possible, and by the time the new ball was taken they had already added 44 runs, Vaughan having hit four boundaries and Cork one.

To begin with it looked as if Adams' strategy had gone badly wrong when 10 runs came from McLean's first over and a further 8 from his own, but Hick, growing in confidence and now with a half-century to his name, danced down the wicket to be beaten by the turning ball. Jacobs had ample time to remove the bails, and Hick was not even close to regaining his ground.

Hick st Jacobs b Adams 59
Vaughan n.o. 45 England 222 - 7

Craig White defended the remainder of the over safely, and then, after Vaughan took a single, found himself facing McLean. But the man who had so far been a hero with the ball was to prove a failure with the bat, at least in this match: he nicked a ball outside off stump and Jacobs took an easy catch.

White c Jacobs b McLean 0
Vaughan n.o. 46 England 223 - 8

Craig White

143

Adams to Hick

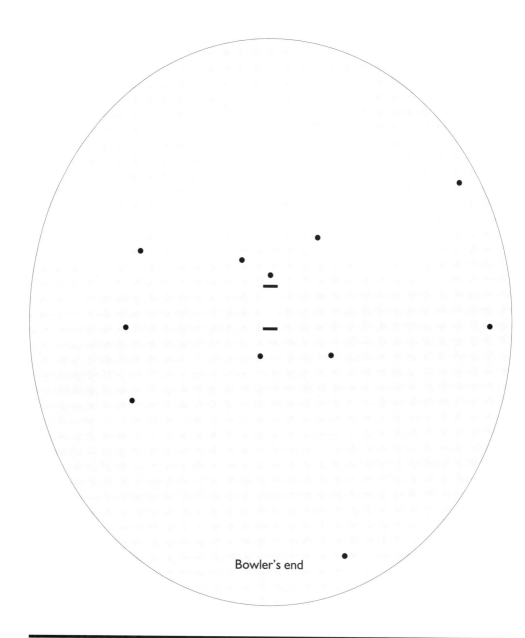

Bowler's end

Adams' field for Hick (left-arm slow, right-hand bat)

Hick 59 not out

England 222 -6

Ambrose took the new ball at the earliest opportunity. His first ball was a no-ball off which Cork took a single, but the next was an away-swinger which took the edge of Vaughan's bat, and Jacobs once more took the catch.

At last Gough did make contact, but he only succeeded in hitting the ball high on the off side where Griffith, fielding at point, took the catch which ended the England innings. Their lead was exactly 100.

Vaughan c Jacobs b Ambrose 76
Cork n.o. 10 England 269 - 9

Gough c Griffith b Walsh 2
Cork n.o. 11 England 272 all out

The ninth-wicket partnership had been a very valuable one for England, perhaps even a match-winning one, with excellent batting based on a sound appraisal of the circumstances. England's lead was now almost 100, and, although it would be nice to have a few more runs to play with, there was not really any pressure on Gough to perform well with the bat.

That was just as well, because Cork and Gough now threw the bat at everything, and rarely made contact.

Twelve overs remained to be bowled before the tea interval, and the West Indies openers needed to make sure that they were still together when the interval arrived. The deficit on first innings was 100, but, although the pitch was helpful to the bowlers, Hick and Vaughan had shown that it was possible to make runs on it, and with judicious batting, the West Indies should be just about on level terms, or even in the lead, at close of play. Their aim must be to get there with as many wickets intact as possible.

The ever-alert West Indian slip cordon

England on the other hand were in a very strong position, and would be able to mount an all-out attack, certainly until tea and probably well beyond. Their major objective would be to get Lara to the crease as quickly as possible, and then to send him back to the pavilion before he had a chance to settle into a match-saving innings, which everyone knew he was capable of doing.

Gough and Caddick opened the bowling and, with Campbell taking a single from the last ball of Gough's over and then playing out a maiden from Caddick, it was not until the third over that Adrian Griffith faced the bowling. But he played a loose shot to the first ball he received, the ball passed between bat and pad, and knocked his off stump out of the ground.

Griffith b Gough 0
Campbell n.o. 3 West Indies 3 - 1

Griffith was replaced by Wavell Hinds, whose first ball was a beautiful delivery which hit him on the back pad, and umpire Cowie had no hesitation in giving him out.

Hinds lbw b Gough 0
Campbell n.o. 3 West Indies 3 - 2

The West Indies could not have imagined a worse start, nor England a better one, and the first part of England's plan vis-à-vis Lara, that of getting him to the crease early, had come to fruition. Not only that, but Gough was on a hat-trick.

But Lara defended the hat-trick ball comfortably and then took a single off the next ball. The next delivery to Campbell went very fine for four off his thigh pad, but the runs were credited to the batsman, so the umpire at least thought he had got some bat on it.

England's slip cordon

The next over from Caddick was fairly uneventful, but when Lara once again faced Gough he looked as if he was intending to mount a counter-attack, cutting the ball very hard but not managing to penetrate the field.

Then he received a ball which pitched on line and straightened; it took Lara on his pads as he tried to leave it, and once more umpire Cowie raised his finger. Gough had struck again, and England's wish to dismiss Lara early had been fulfilled.

Lara lbw b Gough 2
Campbell n.o. 8 West Indies 11 - 3

Jimmy Adams

It was probably not until this point that it crossed anyone's mind that we could be in for a repetition of the Lord's scenario, which would mean an innings win for England. Certainly the West Indies were now in deep trouble, still 89 runs short of making England bat again and with three of their best batsmen gone. The absolute necessity of not losing another wicket before tea was now uppermost in West Indian minds; beyond that, they would have to wait and see – there were, after all, still three days left to play after this one.

But there still remained a lot of work for England to do, and Adams was capable of solid resistance, as England had seen already in the series. Moreover they had not been able to get Sarwan out in the first innings, and the young man was growing in confidence and in stature. Another six overs went by, and the tea interval was in sight; only ten runs had been added, but every run at this stage was valuable, and the bowling had been exceptionally good – not only from Gough, who had taken all three wickets to have fallen so far, but from Caddick, who had taken none.

Then Gough, continuing to probe just outside Campbell's off stump made him edge a ball which flew very low to the right of Hick at second slip. It would have been a difficult catch anyway, but the fact that Thorpe dived across in front of Hick in an attempt to catch it himself made it especially difficult, and it was amazing that Hick was able to hold it.

Campbell c Hick b Gough 12
Adams n.o. 3 West Indies 21 - 4

Campbell was now replaced by Sarwan, and he and Adams successfully negotiated the remaining nine balls before tea.

Tea interval: West Indies 22 - 4
Adams n.o. 4 Sarwan n.o. 0

The tea interval came at a good time for the English bowlers too, for it enabled Gough and Caddick to continue for longer than would otherwise have been the case.

Dominic Cork

Gough carried on as he had left off, but Caddick tried one over attacking Adams's leg stump, but with no success. Gough, who was swinging the ball prodigiously, had Sarwan in all sorts of trouble, but the moment he dropped one short the young West Indian pulled him to long leg for four.

Cork then came on in place of Caddick, and showed that he too could swing the ball. Then Gough started attacking Adams' off stump, hoping to induce the same mistake that had led to his downfall in the first innings. Twice Adams was tempted, and twice the ball raced to the boundary, but conceding runs was less important to England than taking wickets at this stage, and as long as he kept playing that shot Adams was going to give them a chance.

Then Nasser Hussain decided to bring back Caddick, but this time from the Football Ground end, the end from which Gough had done all the damage so far. But it was Cork who had the first success. Having first of all bruised Adams on the finger, which involved fairly lengthy medical attention, he gave Adams another chance to drive outside off stump. This time the ploy worked; in a carbon copy of his first innings dismissal Adams dragged the ball back on to his stumps.

Adams b Cork 19
Sarwan n.o. 10 West Indies 49 - 5

Caddick and Cork continued to bowl superbly, and then, with the first ball

Andrew Caddick

of the 23rd over of the innings, Caddick bowled a delivery that pitched in line with the stumps and straightened, and umpire Cowie gave Jacobs out lbw. It was perhaps a little hard on Jacobs, for there was perhaps reason to think that the ball might have passed over the stumps, but the umpire's finger went up, so Jacobs had to go.

Jacobs lbw b Caddick 1
Sarwan n.o. 12 West Indies 52 - 6

McLean came in, and the first ball he received ballooned up to Vaughan at short leg, to the delight of the crowd – but it had come off pad, not bat. The next ball, however, was a different matter; it was a superb delivery that passed between bat and pad and knocked McLean's off stump out of the ground.

McLean b Caddick 0
Sarwan n.o. 12 West Indies 52 - 7

Out came Curtly Ambrose, and in he went again, as Caddick bowled an identical ball which had the identical result.

Ambrose b Caddick 0
Sarwan n.o. 12 West Indies 52 - 8

So three wickets in four balls for Caddick, and the possibility of a hat-trick too. The field Nasser Hussain set for King was unbelievable: five slips, two gullies, forward short leg and backward square leg. The hat-trick ball was too good for King, but passed harmlessly outside off stump. The next ball was a no-ball, but the person to regret that in the end was the batsman rather than the bowler, for Caddick then bowled an in-swinging yorker that removed his off stump.

King b Caddick 0
Sarwan n.o. 12 West Indies 53 - 9

Another wicket for Caddick

Caddick to King

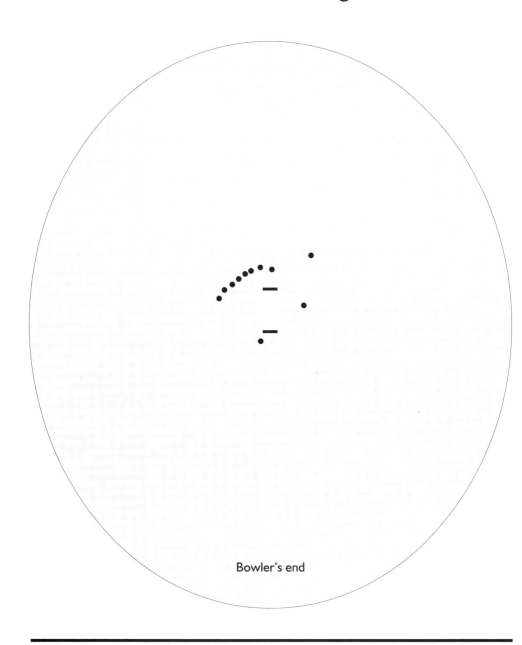

Bowler's end

Caddick's field for King (right-arm fast, right-hand bat)

King 0 not out (hat-trick ball)

West Indies 52 - 8

The last man, Courtney Walsh, came to the crease, no doubt relieved that Caddick's over was finished. Now normal service was resumed, with poor Sarwan, who had looked on incredulously at the other end at the carnage perpetrated by Caddick, continuing to play not only impeccably but positively, and he played a sparkling cover drive off Cork for four.

What options now remained for the West Indies? Precious few, although rain was in the air, and the weather forecast was not good either for the rest of the day or for the weekend. But three days continuous rain is perhaps a little too much to hope for, and it was unrealistic in cricketing terms to think that the West Indies had any chance of saving the match.

Courtney Walsh takes guard

So Walsh played a few wild swings, and then a very elegant shot off his toes for three, but before long – inevitably – he saw his off stump uprooted by a full length ball from Caddick, who had now taken 5 wickets for 14 runs.

Walsh b Caddick 3
Sarwan n.o. 17
West Indies 61 all out
England won by an innings and 39 runs

So the match ended well inside two days – the first time this had happened in England since 1921, and only the fourteenth time out of 1508 test in the entire history of test cricket.

What enabled England to win? Was the pitch so bad? The answer must be that the pitch was helpful to the bowlers, but Thorpe, Vaughan, Hick and Sarwan all showed that it was possible to make runs on it. In addition it was swing through the air rather than movement off the pitch which helped the England bowlers, i.e. atmospheric conditions, and they exploited the conditions very well, aided and abetted, it has to be said, by some indifferent batting on the part of the West Indies. But what undoubtedly tipped the balance of the match were the partnerships between first Vaughan and Hick and then Vaughan and Cork, which led to Michael Vaughan being named man of the match. During the presentation ceremony, ten minutes after the match ended... it began to rain.

Match Scorecard

West Indies	First Innings		Second Innings	
Campbell	c Trescothick b Gough	8	c Hick b Gough	12
Griffith	c Stewart b Gough	22	b Gough	0
Hinds	c Stewart b White	16	lbw b Gough	0
Lara	lbw b White	4	lbw b Gough	2
Adams	b White	2	b Cork	19
Sarwan	not out	59	not out	17
Jacobs	c Caddick b Cork	35	lbw b Caddick	1
McLean	c Stewart b White	7	b Caddick	0
Ambrose	b Cork	1	b Caddick	0
King	lbw b Gough	6	b Caddick	0
Walsh	c Caddick b White	1	b Caddick	3
Extras	lb 2, nb 9	11	lb3, nb4	7
Total	(48.4 overs, 218 min)	172	(26.2 overs, 127 min)	61

Fall of wickets:
First innings: 1-11, 2-50, 3-54, 4-56, 5-60, 6-128, 7-143, 8-148, 9-168
Second innings: 1-3, 2-3, 3-11, 4-21, 5-49, 6-52, 7-52, 8-52, 9-53
Bowling:
Gough 17-2-59-3, Caddick 10-3-35-0
White 14.4-4-57-5, Cork 7-0-19-2

Gough 10-3-30-4, Caddick 11.2-5-14-5
Cork 5-0-14-1

England	First Innings	
Atherton	c Lara b Ambrose	6
Trescothick	c Lara b Ambrose	1
Hussain	lbw b Walsh	22
Thorpe	lbw b Walsh	46
Stewart	c Campbell b Walsh	5
Vaughan	c Jacobs b Ambrose	76
Caddick	c Jacobs b Ambrose	6
Hick	st Jacobs b Adams	59
White	c Jacobs b McLean	0
Cork	not out	11
Gough	c Griffith b Walsh	2
Extras	b4, lb 13, w3, nb 18	38
Total	(81.5 overs, 360 min)	272

Fall of wickets:
First innings: 1-7, 2-10, 3-80, 4-93, 5-96, 6-124, 7-222, 8-223, 9-269

Bowling
Ambrose 18-3-42-4, Walsh 24.5-9-51-4
King 11-2-48-0, McLean 22-5-93-1
Adams 6-1-21-1

England won by an innings and 93 runs

The Fifth Test

The Oval

Background

Both sides went into this final match of the series wanting desperately to win. The West Indies knew that winning the series was now beyond them, but at least a win would enable them not only to level the series at 2 - 2 with one match drawn, but also give them and their supporters some hope for the future as their leading bowlers Ambrose and Walsh contemplated retirement.

England knew that they would win the series even if the match were drawn, but wanted a win in order to emphasise not only their superiority in this series but also their re-emergence as a force to be reckoned with. Moreover this would be England's first series win against the West Indies since 1969, and there would be a feeling that if they could not win a series against this transitional West Indian side, they probably never would again.

The Weather

The first day started in sunshine, but there was no guarantee that the fine weather would be maintained, and conditions might well become overcast, and it was thought unlikely that the match would be completed without being interrupted by rain at some stage in the proceedings.

The Pitch

The Oval pitch these days is by no means as fast as it was, for instance, when Devon Malcolm bowled out the South Africans in 1994. At the start of this match this was undoubtedly the driest pitch of the series, although it was quite grassy in parts. It is a pitch that tends to take spin, but it is worthy of note that although the Surrey spinners Saqlain Mushtaq and Ian Salisbury have had a lot of success there of late, visiting spinners have been much less successful.

Team Selection

The West Indies were obliged to make at least one change because Reon King was injured, as was Franklyn Rose, so it was easy for them to find a place in their line-up for the leg-spinner Mahendra Nagamootoo, who would be playing in his first test. This, however, was their only change.

England surprised most commentators by not including a specialist spinner. It would, however, have been difficult for England to leave out a member of the side which had won so comprehensively at Headingley. With Dominic Cork having made a double century for his county since the events of Headingley, the England side had an unusual depth to their batting.

Umpires Shepherd and Harper

England	West Indies
Atherton	Campbell
Trescothick	Griffith
Hussain (Capt)	Hinds
Thorpe	Lara
Stewart (Wkt)	Adams (Capt)
Vaughan	Sarwan
Hick	Jacobs (Wkt)
White	Nagamootoo
Cork	Ambrose
Caddick	McLean
Gough	Walsh

Umpires: D. Shepherd & D. Harper

The Toss

Jimmy Adams won the toss for the fourth time in the series and the third time in succession. Once more his decision was controversial: he opted to bowl first, feeling that if there was to be any help in this pitch for his bowlers it would probably be on the first morning rather than later. But the inclusion of Nagamootoo meant that the West Indies were better equipped to take advantage of the likely conditions later in the match than were England. Most observers felt that Adams had made a mistake, and Nasser Hussain claimed that he would have batted first anyway.

Immediate Aims

The England players knew that the West Indies needed to win this match since a draw would mean that they would lose the series. It was therefore essential for them to make a solid start; as commentator Barry Richards said on television, you can never win a match in the first session, but you can lose it. If Jimmy Adams's assessment of the pitch were right, he would be disappointed not to take two or three wickets before lunch; England's prime objective then was to ensure that Adams was disappointed.

The First Day

Ambrose and Walsh opened the proceedings, and Ambrose, on target right away, began his spell with two maidens to Atherton. Walsh, not to be outdone, also found his line and length straight away, and he bowled two maidens to Trescothick. It was not until the last ball of the fifth over that a run was scored, when Atherton took a single off Ambrose with a defensive push towards the vacant mid-on area. The next scoring shot, off Walsh's next over, was somewhat fortuitous, as Atherton edged a ball – but not at catchable height – between first and second slip to the boundary. The next four overs then produced only two runs, and after ten overs had been bowled England's score was still only 7 for 0. A firm push by Trescothick to the mid-wicket boundary off the first ball of Ambrose's next over was the first really attacking shot of the England innings.

Then Walsh was removed from the attack to be replaced by McLean. In the earlier matches of the series this would have meant an immediate increase in the English scoring rate, but on this occasion McLean emulated the accuracy of his senior colleagues, and only one run was taken off his first over.

Ambrose's next over was yet another maiden, although four runs were added to the total when the ball flew off Atherton's thigh pad and went between wicket-keeper and first slip for four leg-byes. Then Trescothick decided it was time to attack McLean, and scored two boundaries in four

A section of the enthusiastic crowd

balls. He was in fact a trifle fortunate, because Campbell fielding at second slip managed to get his finger tips to the first of these shots as it passed over his head but was unable to hold it; a taller player might well have been able to bring off the catch and secure the wicket which West Indies so badly needed.

Most of the morning's play followed the same pattern; the ball passed the bat now and again, but when it did take an edge it fell safely to ground. Occasionally the ball hit a pad, but never in such a position that either batsman was in danger of being given out. Every now and again the ball went for four, sometimes deliberately sometimes fortuitously. But still no wicket fell.

Ambrose was replaced by Walsh, and the pattern looked set to continue, but then, after only 39 runs had been scored from 22 overs, 21 came in three overs – unusually, 16 from two overs from Walsh. But then all went quiet again, as Nagamootoo was introduced from the Vauxhall end, and the last four overs before lunch only yielded six runs.

Lunch : England 66 - 0
Atherton n.o. 30
Trescothick n.o. 30

So England weathered the early storm, such as it was. The West Indian bowlers had achieved good movement and bounce in the early stages, and had bowled very accurately as usual, but the pitch was not really very helpful to them, and the English batsmen, with a combination of good luck and good judgment in knowing when to leave and when to play, had ensured that their first objective was achieved: they had reached lunch without losing a wicket. There had been only 26 scoring strokes during the course of the morning's 29 overs, but the ball had reached the boundary eleven times.

England now had a platform on which they could build, and simply needed to be patient; time was on their side, and as the ball got older and the pitch got flatter the runs should come more easily. Jimmy Adams had more of a problem. His opening bowlers had taken no wickets so far, which meant he was in fairly unfamiliar territory. But Walsh and Ambrose probably remained his best chance of making a breakthrough.

Another interested spectator

His answer was to persevere with Nagamootoo and Walsh, but, although Walsh once more bowled impeccably, with four maidens out of his first five overs after lunch, Atherton and Trescothick had little problem keeping the scoreboard ticking over, each hitting the spinner elegantly to the boundary – one shot by Trescothick through mid-off was particularly impressive as he managed to spot Nagamootoo's googly early.

Eight overs into the afternoon Ambrose returned to the attack, and he and Walsh continued in tandem for seven overs, but the nearest the West Indies came to taking a wicket was when Atherton took a quick single to Adams, who picked up and shied at the stumps in one movement; a direct hit would have sent Trescothick on his way back to the pavilion, but the throw missed. Walsh eventually left the attack when Trescothick smashed him twice to the cover boundary off consecutive deliveries; the first of these boundaries took Trescothick to his fifty and the opening partnership to three figures.

Ambrose continued for a further three overs, whilst McLean replaced Walsh; when Ambrose needed a rest Jimmy Adams brought back Nagamootoo. But it made no difference, and Trescothick and Atherton continued relentlessly – not flashy but efficient. As tea approached Adams decided it was time for spin at both ends, and brought himself on to bowl at the Pavilion end. Just as it seemed that

England would have batted for two whole sessions without losing a wicket, Trescothick edged a ball from Nagamootoo to Campbell at slip. At first he appeared to have missed it, but he turned and took the catch somewhere behind his right ear. It was a great reflex catch, exactly what the West Indies needed, and it gave young Nagamootoo his first wicket in test cricket.

Trescothick c Campbell
b Nagamootoo 78
Atherton n.o. 71 England 159 - 1

Shortly before that Trescothick and Atherton had established a new opening partnership record for West Indian matches at the Oval, surpassing the achievements of Boycott and Gooch (1980) and Hobbs and Sutcliffe (1928). As there were only three balls remaining before the scheduled tea break the players now left the field.

Tea Interval: England 159 - 1
Atherton n.o. 71
Hussain yet to come in

The *Test Match Special* box

Nagamootoo to Thorpe

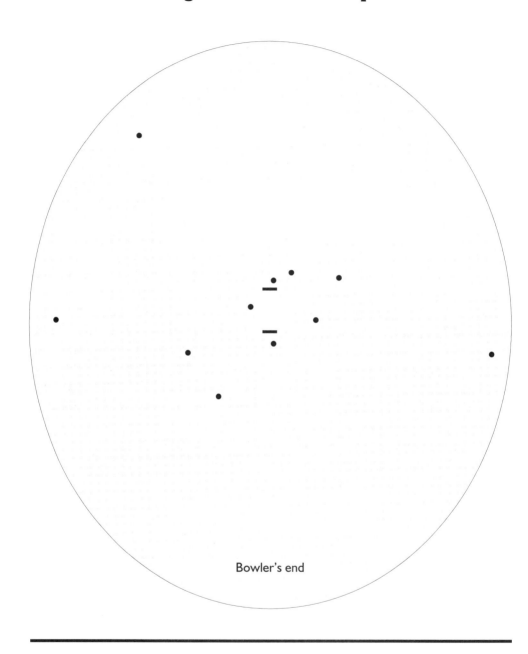

Bowler's end

Nagamootoo's field for Thorpe (right-arm leg-break, left-hand bat)

Thorpe I not out

England 167 - 2

The West Indies were still not in the sort of position their captain had hoped for when he decided to ask England to bat first, but they would be a good deal happier now they had taken a wicket. What is more, a wicket taken immediately before an interval often seems to motivate a side more than one taken in mid-session. They knew that the next man in was Nasser Hussain, who was having a miserable season with the bat, and if they could get him out, and then take two or three more wickets fairly quickly, particularly towards the end of the day when the new ball was due, they would feel they were back in the match. Nearly all the matches played in the series so far had seen swings of fortune, so there was no reason to suppose that things would not shortly be going their way. As for England, they simply needed to keep on building; Atherton was still there, and the depth of batting they had meant that they could afford now to start trying to push the score along, their object being to score well over 300 if not more.

– and another spot for Angus Fraser

Professional cricketers will often say, as they try to encourage each other 'one wicket brings two', and so it proved now, as Nasser Hussain snicked the second ball he received to the wicket-keeper.

Hussain c Jacobs b McLean 0
Atherton n.o. 71 England 159 - 2

Walsh now came on to join Nagamootoo, and inevitably began his new spell by bowling a maiden over to Atherton, but the next eight overs brought no further success to the West Indian bowlers, so Jimmy Adams turned to Nixon McLean. McLean too bowled a maiden, this time to Thorpe, and then, with the first ball of his next over, he got the wicket the West Indies most desperately wanted: he generated a little extra pace, the ball jagged back inside Atherton's angled bat, and took the top of middle stump.

Atherton b McLean 83
Thorpe n.o. 8 England 184 - 3

So Alec Stewart came out on his home ground to join his county colleague Graham Thorpe – but not for long, because, on the third ball he received, Stewart took a big stride across his stumps, appeared to slip slightly, and was hit on the pads right in front of his middle stump.

Stewart lbw b McLean 0
Thorpe n.o. 8 England 184 - 4

Vaughan, the man of the match at Headingley, now came in and quickly got off the mark with two good boundaries off McLean. With Thorpe playing confidently too, it now looked as if England were set to recover from their temporary setback, and before long the England score had reached 200.

What was particularly unusual about the England scorecard at this stage was that, of the four wickets down, not one had yet fallen to either Ambrose or Walsh. But the new ball was due fairly soon, and with only ten overs left in the day's play if the new ball were taken after the statutory 80 overs, Ambrose and Walsh would still have a virtually new ball to bowl with the following morning as well.

But Jimmy Adams did not take the new ball yet, possibly because Nagamootoo was getting some turn. The appearance of the old ball, however, suggested another reason: although it was more than eighty overs old it had still retained a good shine. Since it was still swinging well, there was no need to take the new ball yet. The reason for this was almost certainly because the outfield at the Oval is quite lush because of the installation of pop-up sprinklers; hitting the ball to the boundary does not therefore have the abrasive effect on the ball that is found on most grounds.

Ambrose came back into the attack and, still bowling with the old ball, brought one back from outside the off stump. Vaughan shouldered arms and was hit on the pad, and umpire Shepherd had no hesitation in raising his finger.

Vaughan lbw b Ambrose 10
Thorpe n.o. 28 England 214 - 5

Nagamootoo continued at the Vauxhall end, and bowled a maiden to Thorpe, thus ensuring that Ambrose was able to continue bowling at the newcomer, Graeme Hick. Hick did manage to score two down to third man thanks to a fumble by Walsh, but was not very comfortable as Ambrose was swinging the ball both ways, and he was perhaps a trifle lucky to survive a big lbw appeal.

Nagamootoo

Walsh then took over from Nagamootoo – perhaps because Nagamootoo was taking less than 1½ minutes to bowl an over and the veteran Ambrose needed more rest in between overs – but still the new ball was not taken. But it was getting gradually darker and darker, and eventually, with only two balls of the 90th over of the day remaining, the umpires decided that the light was too bad to continue.

Close of play: England 221 - 5 Thorpe n.o. 31 Hick n.o. 2

The Second Day

The weather forecasters were not very optimistic about the weather for the second day, but play started on time under a fairly clear sky and bright sunshine. Both teams' coaches professed themselves satisfied with the situation at the end of the first day, although an independent observer would probably feel that England had a slight advantage at this stage. Much would depend upon the first session, however. The West Indies needed to take the remaining English wickets quickly if they were to maintain a realistic chance of winning the match; getting England out by lunch would probably be their aim. England, of course, would be aiming to bat for as long as possible and to build up as big a score as they could.

Walsh began by bowling the remaining two balls of the previous day's unfinished over. Ambrose then took the new ball, despite the fact that Walsh had just demonstrated that the old ball was still swinging well. One run came from each of the next two overs, and then Ambrose bowled a maiden to Hick who, although he survived, experienced some difficulty doing so. The surprise was that no close fielder was brought in on the leg side to take advantage of Hick's discomfiture with balls coming in towards his legs.

An even bigger surprise was that Nixon McLean then came on to relieve Courtney Walsh after the latter had bowled only one over with the new ball. The reason was probably that Jimmy Adams wanted to avoid bowling Ambrose and Walsh in tandem so he could almost always have one or the other of them operating. In earlier matches this had not been possible because the support bowling had been so poor, but the fact that McLean bowled so well on the first day of this match would encourage Adams to feel it was worth employing this tactic.

Both Ambrose and McLean did bowl well, and runs were hard to come by, but seven overs into the day's play the rain which had been forecast finally materialised, and the players left the field. Only nine runs had been added during those seven overs.

Rain stopped play: England 230 - 5 Thorpe n.o. 31 Hick n.o. 7

Fortunately the strong breeze which had brought in the rain clouds so quickly dispatched them with equal alacrity, and play was only delayed by eleven minutes. When play resumed,

Ambrose and McLean continued their attack. Batting remained difficult, and both bowlers were unlucky, hitting pads, making both batsmen play and miss, and McLean was probably especially unlucky not to get the verdict when he appealed for a catch by Ridley Jacobs against Thorpe, for television replays suggested he might have got the thinnest of edges, but in truth it would have been virtually impossible for an umpire to detect so fine an edge with the naked eye.

Walsh then came back into the attack, and still runs were slow in coming; ten overs had passed before Thorpe scored his first run of the day. But the score crept up bit by bit, and the England total soon passed 250 – but the last fifty runs had not included a single boundary.

Then Ambrose bowled a bouncer at Hick; it was not a very high one, and Hick ducked, resisting the temptation to hook because Ambrose had put a man at deep square leg and another at deep fine leg. This was followed by an identical delivery, and Hick ducked again. The third ball was on a good length, and angled in towards Hick, just missing the outside edge. The next two deliveries were also on target, but Hick managed to keep them out, but the final ball of the over was dead straight, and Hick was caught plumb lbw.

Hick lbw b Ambrose 17
Thorpe n.o. 40 England 254 - 6

Walsh was now the only front-line bowler not to have taken a wicket – a most unusual circumstance – and he was determined not to be left out. With the fifth ball of his next over he tried once more the slower ball that had embarrassed Thorpe at Old Trafford, and achieved the identical result, with Thorpe turning towards the pavilion even before the umpire's finger went up.

Thorpe lbw b Walsh 40
White n.o. 0 England 254 - 7

England now had two newcomers at the crease, and the West Indies were possibly on target as far as dismissing England before lunch was concerned. Two overs and one run later McLean returned to replace Ambrose. His first ball beat Cork completely, and rapped him on the pads; he appealed, but the appeal was turned down. Cork then tried hard to get off the mark from each of the next three balls, but

The West Indian wicket keeper featured on the Oval's big screen

without success. Then McLean produced a perfectly straight ball and achieved the fifth lbw dismissal of the innings; it was an almost identical delivery to the one with which Ambrose dismissed Graeme Hick.

Cork lbw b McLean 0
White n.o. 1 England 255 - 8

So England had gone from 254 for 5 to 255 for 8; they had lost three wickets so far in the morning's play but only scored 34 runs. The decline looked even worse when one looked at the position immediately before tea on the first day, when the score was 159 for no wicket. The West Indies had certainly bowled their way back into the match, and they had done it by dint of maintaining a perfect line and length, without too many of the loose deliveries which had been the hallmark of their support bowlers' performance in the earlier tests.

White and Caddick ensured that no further wicket fell before lunch, although without adding to the score. Ominously, rain was falling as the players left the field for lunch.

Lunch interval: England 255 - 8
White n.o. 1 Caddick n.o. 0

So the West Indians had not managed to take the remaining English wickets before lunch, but, given that there had been a rain break and England had only scored 34 runs in the session, they would feel that they had effectively done better than they had hoped. They would now expect to finish the innings off within a very short space of time, and then get some way towards matching the England total by the end of the day.

But to the disappointment of everyone, only eleven balls were possible after lunch before the rain came once more, and the players again left the field.

Ian McLaurin and John Major – but the champagne's for later!

Rain stopped play: England 256 - 8
White n.o. 2 Caddick n.o. 0

It was not possible for play to resume until 3.35, which would be more disappointing for the West Indians than for England, because the best part of two days had now gone and the English first innings was not yet over. When play did resume, it was clear that the English batsmen had decided to go for quick runs, and Caddick played a beautiful square drive off a short ball from Walsh which produced the first boundary of the day – in fact the first boundary since before 5 o'clock on the first day. White then pulled a short delivery from McLean, but mistimed it, and the ball flew high towards the vacant mid-wicket area. Hinds, fielding close in on the leg side made a valiant effort to reach it, but was not quite able to get there in time, and two runs were added to the score.

It was fairly predictable that before long one of the bowlers would respond to this willingness to swing the bat by bowling a bouncer and inviting a hook, and this is indeed what happened. The bowler was Walsh, the batsman Caddick; Caddick hooked, but hit the ball with glove rather than bat, and this time Hinds was able to take a fairly easy catch at leg gully.

Caddick c Hinds b Walsh 4
White n.o. 6 England 264 - 9

Darren Gough now came to the crease, and hoisted a ball from McLean to the mid-wicket boundary – rather

Andy Caddick

an inelegant-looking shot, but effective. In the next over, after Gough had been tucked up by a bouncer from Walsh, three quick singles were taken, followed by another boundary, this time a square cut by Craig White. But it was to be Walsh who had the last word; in his next over he sent down a quicker, straight ball, and removed Gough's off stump. But the last-wicket partnership had been quite effective: White and Gough had added 17 runs in 26 balls, whereas it had taken Thorpe and Hick 70 balls to score the same number of runs at the beginning of the day. As the players left the field, rain began to fall once more.

Gough b Walsh 8
White n.o. 11 England 281 all out

Tea was taken at this stage, but rain continued to fall during this time, and it was not possible to resume play until 5.50, only ten minutes short of the normal time for close of play. In theory 21 overs remained to be bowled, but although the sun was shining when the players took the field again, it always seemed unlikely that play would continue for as long as that.

But however long this session was to last, it would inevitably be a difficult time for the West Indies; they would not have time to make much progress towards matching the England total, but they could easily lose a couple of wickets in the process, and thus put themselves under great pressure on the following day.

Gough and Caddick opened the bowling to Campbell and Griffith, and as play got under way, it was almost a mirror image of the England innings, with batsmen playing and missing, edges not quite carrying to fielders, close lbw calls, and very few runs being scored; in fact the first four overs were maidens, and it was not until the last ball of the ninth over that Campbell got

Brian Lara

the ball to the boundary, and that was off the edge along the ground between third slip and gully. That took the score to 9 off nine overs.

In fact only five further overs were possible because the light gradually deteriorated, and the West Indian batsmen would ultimately have been very relieved to make their way back to the pavilion without having lost a wicket.

Close of play: West Indies 13 - 0 Campbell n.o. 6 Griffith n.o. 4

The Third Day

At the start of play on the third day both sides' objectives would be much as they were at the start of the West Indian innings. The West Indian batsmen would have to make a fresh start, and would want to try and stay at the crease for as long as possible, preferably until lunch-time. England would be particularly keen to take a wicket early on, and as usual would feel that Brian Lara held the key to the final outcome.

The weather was significantly better than on the previous day, although there had been heavy rain earlier in the morning. It was however possible to start on time, and there was even a promise of sunshine at some stage.

Gough began by bowling a no-ball to Griffith, but apart from that his opening over was a maiden, as was Caddick's to Campbell.

At this point the sun made a welcome appearance. The ball was beating the bat fairly regularly at this stage. The edges of both bats were much in evidence, and when a boundary came to Campbell off Caddick in the fourth over of the day it was not surprisingly an edge which flew over the heads of the slips.

It was clearly the England strategy to bowl a full length and invite the batsmen to drive, in the hope of inducing catches off the edge, and the field was set accordingly, with some inviting gaps in front of the wicket. It is a strategy that can be expensive in terms of giving away runs, but in these circumstances, with the ball swinging a good deal, it seemed to be the right approach.

The Oval crowd all turn to watch a replay on the big screen

That meant, as can be seen in the diagram, that Andy Caddick had three slips, two gullies, cover, fine-leg, silly mid-on and mid-wicket.

The result was indeed an increase in the scoring rate, and Campbell quickly moved on to 20 with some good-looking shots, especially an off-drive off Caddick which went for four.

Craig White now came on to replace Darren Gough at the pavilion end, and bowled a good opening over to Griffith, who had had little of the strike so far. Then Nasser Hussain brought on Cork at the Vauxhall end. His first ball to Campbell swung away towards the slips, but Campbell left it alone. His second was pitched on off stump and was played defensively. His third swung, came back off the seam, and then scattered Campbell's stumps by way of the inside edge as he tried to drive Cork away on the off side.

Campbell b Cork 20
Griffith n.o. 6 West Indies 32 - 1

Wavell Hinds came to take Campbell's place, but did not need to play a shot at any of the remaining balls of Cork's over. It was the same with the first three balls of White's next over, but then Griffith tried to drive a full length delivery just outside the off stump and gave a catch off the outside edge to Hick at second slip.

Griffith c Hick b White 6
Hinds n.o. 0 West Indies 32 - 2

Caddick to Campbell

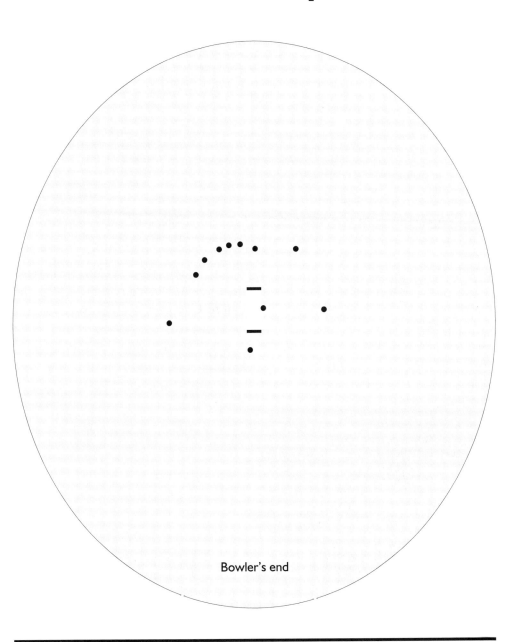

Bowler's end

Caddick's field for Campbell (right-arm fast, right-hand bat)

Campbell 6 not out

West Indies 15 - 0

In came Brian Lara. Craig White bowled him another full length ball, Lara moved across his stumps, and the ball removed his leg stump. White said in an interview afterwards that he had noticed in earlier innings that Lara had a habit of moving across to the off side and leaving his leg stump exposed, and he had always intended to try and exploit that as soon as Lara came to the wicket. It was a classic case of getting a reward for doing one's homework properly. Moreover it was the first time Brian Lara had ever been dismissed first ball in test cricket.

Lara b White 0
Hinds n.o. 0 West Indies 32 - 3

Jimmy Adams survived the hat-trick ball from White, the last ball of the over, and then it was Hinds' turn to face Cork. The first delivery was

As has been stressed before, cricket is very much a psychological game, and the psychological effect on both sides of a batsman such as Lara being out first ball is tremendous. It puts an extra spring in the step of the fielders, it adds a yard of pace to the fast bowlers, and it also requires intense concentration and discipline from the batting side if they are to avoid falling prey to a sort of collective hysteria and become totally incapable of batting in their normal fashion – and both of these sides have shown that that can happen quite easily.

The fact that three wickets had fallen without the score advancing at all would tend to increase that danger for the West Indies, and it was now imperative that their batsmen should buckle down and ensure that no further mishaps befell them.

Cork appeals for leg before wicket

outside off stump, and Hinds ignored it. Then Hinds got off the mark, turning the ball off his legs for two, but the third ball swung back towards him, took him on the pad, and he too was out.

Hinds lbw b Cork 2
Adams n.o. 0 West Indies 34 - 4

Ramnaresh Sarwan then came to join his captain. He defended his first ball and then turned Cork to fine leg for a single, thus keeping the strike. After three defensive shots he then drove White to mid-on; the ball did not quite reach the rope, but the batsmen were able to run four. After leaving the next ball to pass harmlessly by off stump, Sarwan then played another drive, but the ball held back a bit, and his drive, off the full face of the bat, flew to gully, where Trescothick took a tremendous catch.

Sarwan c Trescothick b White 5
Adams n.o. 0 West Indies 39 - 5

So half the West Indian side was already out and they were still 242 runs behind. Four overs and a drinks interval now passed, and another all-run four by Jacobs off White had helped the score along to 47. Just as it seemed that the West Indies might be beginning to recover their equilibrium, with Jacobs pushing Cork into the covers for one, and then Adams taking two off a similar shot, Cork reaped the reward for his constant probing outside off stump. After bowling two short deliveries which Adams declined to hook, he bowled another full length ball which swung away late; Adams followed it, and almost patted it into the hands of Hick at second slip.

Adams c Hick b Cork 5
Jacobs n.o. 7 West Indies 51 - 6

When your side's in trouble, just lie back and think of the Caribbean...

West Indies now needed 31 runs to avoid the follow on, although this was fairly academic because in the circumstances it was unlikely that Nasser Hussain would enforce it, not least because if the West Indies were to bat as well in their second innings as they had done at Old Trafford, England would not fancy batting last on a wearing pitch against Ambrose and Walsh.

The newcomer to the crease was the debutant Nagamootoo, but he showed few signs of nerves as he first of all took two runs off a yorker from Caddick, who had just replaced White, then two consecutive boundaries on the off side from Cork, followed immediately by a flick over the heads of the leg-side fielders to deep mid-wicket for another three; by this time he had taken 14 runs from his first eight balls in test cricket.

Gough now came on to join Caddick, and quietened Nagamootoo down with a maiden, but in the next over another on-drive off Caddick brought him yet another boundary. But Nagamootoo's counter-attack was not destined to last long, and off the final ball of Gough's next over he played a square drive off the meat of the bat straight at gully, where Trescothick pulled off another tremendous catch.

Nagamootoo
c Trescothick b Gough 18
Jacobs n.o. 12 West Indies 74 - 7

Nagamootoo's place was taken by Ambrose, but as the wicket had fallen to the last ball of the over it was not yet his turn to face the bowling. He got his

Umpire David Shepherd calls for the third umpire to make a run-out decision

chance on the last ball of Caddick's next over after Jacobs had taken a single off the fifth, but he did not last long: he took a wild swing at the first ball he received, was beaten both by the swing and the pace, and was hit on the back leg to become the second lbw victim of the innings and the seventh of the match.

Ambrose lbw b Caddick 0
Jacobs n.o. 13 West Indies 75 - 8

McLean now came to join Jacobs, and it was he who saved the follow-on by hitting a full toss from Gough to the square leg boundary. Five more runs came from the next over, after which lunch was taken with the West Indies still trailing by 195 runs.

Lunch interval: West Indies 86 - 8
Jacobs n.o. 15 McLean n.o. 8

It was now clear that West Indies, barring some extraordinary heroics by Ridley Jacobs and Nixon McLean, were going to end up with a considerable first-innings deficit. The only option open to them at this stage was to try and hit as hard and as often as possible in the hope of reducing that deficit as much as possible, and then relying on some good bowling and a better performance when their turn came to bat again.

England simply had to carry on as they had been doing, even inviting the batsmen to hit, because in that way they would be more likely to get out.

White and Caddick opened the bowling after lunch, and Jacobs started the ball rolling for West Indies with a drive through the covers for four off White's first delivery. A maiden from Caddick followed, but then McLean hit another four off White and three more fours off Caddick's next two overs. McLean was struck on the helmet and then in the midriff by two successive balls from Caddick, but the runs still came thick and fast. McLean and Jacobs had their share of good fortune, but they played some good shots and deserved their luck; what is more, by successful driving Jacobs and McLean forced Caddick to change his length and bowl shorter.

By the time McLean was out, bowled off the inside edge by White, they had

Nixon McLean

added a very valuable 44 runs off 75 balls.

McLean b White 29
Jacobs n.o. 25 West Indies 119 - 9

Even Walsh made a contribution with the bat, notably with a good straight drive for four before, with his very next ball, Craig White flattened his off stump with a fast in-swinger.

Walsh b White 5
Jacobs n.o. 26
West Indies 125 all out

So England took a first innings lead of 156, just ten more than at Old Trafford, when the West Indies went on to score 438 for 7 in their second innings. The West Indies batting performance had been dismal, but at one time it had looked as if the final outcome would be much worse. But the West Indian bowlers should have learned from the morning's play that the ball would swing if it was pitched up, and they had bowlers who were perfectly capable of doing that. If they could only engineer the sort of collapse that had taken place in the England first innings, but without allowing them to have a big opening stand before that, they could still bowl themselves back into the game. England's first aim must be to bat through the remaining twenty overs or so before tea without losing a wicket, because to lose Atherton and Trescothick early could very well be a prelude to such a collapse.

Ambrose opened the bowling from the Pavilion end, but, given the absolute necessity for the West Indies to take wickets and bowl England out quickly, it was rather surprising to find that his field-placings were not especially aggressive. For the first three overs only Atherton faced the bowling, as he took a single from the last ball of the first over and a three off the last ball of the second, bowled by Walsh. After a maiden by Ambrose it was then Trescothick's turn to face Walsh. Trescothick soon got off the mark, edging a ball through the slips to the third man boundary, but he looked far from comfortable in the first over he faced.

England then made very slow progress, scoring 12 from the first eight overs, and then Atherton played a superb hook shot to the boundary off Ambrose. But two balls and another run later, umbrellas started to go up in the crowd, and play was suspended. It was decided to take tea at this stage, so in effect virtually no time was lost for this rain break.

Rain stopped play, tea interval:
England 17 - 0
Atherton n.o. 11
Trescothick n.o. 5

On the resumption Walsh and Ambrose continued, each starting with a maiden. Then, in his second over after tea, Ambrose, bowling round the wicket to the left-hander and probing away on an off-stump-line, produced a beautiful away-swinger, and Marcus

Andrew Caddick watching himself fielding on the big screen

Trescothick was only able to edge it into the safe hands of Brian Lara.

Botham against Australia at Lord's in 1981.

Trescothick c Lara b Ambrose 7
Atherton n.o. 12 England 21 - 1

Hussain lbw b McLean 0
Atherton n.o. 20 England 29 - 2

The England captain now came in, with everyone conscious that he had been desperately out of form. He began, understandably, somewhat nervously, but played one or two good shots without being able to get off the mark. He was probably rather relieved when, five overs after he came to the wicket, Ambrose was taken off and replaced by McLean. But after Atherton had played the second ball of the over square for three, Hussain received a ball that came back in from off and caught him plumb in front of his stumps. The unfortunate England captain had 'bagged a pair' – the first captain of England to do so since Ian

Graham Thorpe then came out, but before he could take guard the players left the field again, initially for bad light, but then rain started again. Fortunately play was interrupted for a very short time on this occasion, and Thorpe came back to face McLean. The first ball he received was a slower ball; no doubt Nixon McLean was conscious of Thorpe's susceptibility in this area, but his slower ball is less effective than Courtney Walsh's, and Thorpe was not deceived by it.

The sun now came out, only to disappear very soon behind a dark cloud, and ten minutes or so later the light deteriorated again and rain began to fall once more. In the meantime, although Walsh had been bowling ever since Thorpe came to the crease, Atherton made sure that Thorpe did not have to face him yet.

Rain stopped play: England 31 - 2 Atherton n.o. 20 Thorpe n.o. 2

This time the break was to be more prolonged, and when the match was resumed only a further 11 overs were possible, plus the four balls remaining from McLean's interrupted over, before bad light brought play once more to a premature end. During this final period Atherton and Thorpe played sensibly against the bowling of Walsh, McLean and Nagamootoo, without any undue alarms and with 25 runs added, the only boundary coming from a firm drive to third man by Atherton off Nagamootoo.

Close of play: England 56 - 2 Atherton n.o. 36 Thorpe n.o. 10

So England had increased their overall lead to 212, and would be well satisfied with their position with two days left to play. They would hope to add a further 150 or even 200 runs by tea on the fourth day, and they would expect to win from that position.

The West Indies would not yet have lost hope; they had already claimed two good wickets, and if they could dismiss Atherton early on Sunday morning they could yet be in with a chance.

The Fourth Day

The sun was shining brightly when play was resumed on the Sunday morning, and despite all the rain that had fallen in the past few days the pitch looked very dry. Ambrose and Walsh opened the attack, and hit on a good line and length straight away, as is their wont, and the day began with three maiden overs. In the fourth over of the day Walsh was bowling to Thorpe, and off the third ball of this over Thorpe played the ball off his legs and gave a catch to Griffith behind square. No runs had yet been added to the overnight score, and this was an ideal start for the West Indies.

Thorpe c Griffith b Walsh 10 Atherton n.o. 36 England 56 - 3

Alec Stewart came in and played out the remainder of Walsh's over, a maiden, which was followed by two further maidens. It was a very intense period of play, with the West Indians not wanting to give away runs but wanting to take wickets and the English batsmen determined to stay in and not worrying too much about runs, and in the first half-hour of the day only two runs were scored from eight overs. The pattern continued for a further half-hour, and when a drinks break was taken after 15 overs, the England total had still only risen to 65; of the nine runs scored this morning, five were extras. What was important for England though was that they had lost no further wicket, and what they

McLean to Atherton

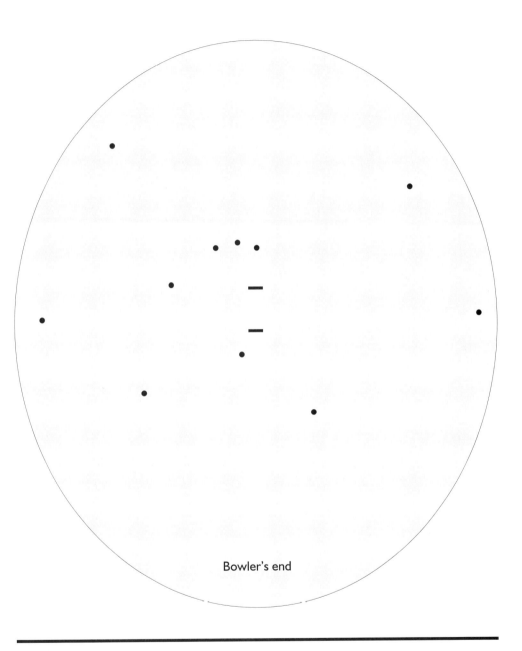

Bowler's end

McLean's field for Atherton (right-arm fast, right-hand bat)

Atherton 24 not out

England 41 - 2

Courtney Walsh

were intent on doing was batting the West Indies out of the game.

A maiden from Walsh to Stewart immediately after the resumption led one to feel that this stalemate would last all day, but then in the next over from McLean Atherton at last punched the ball down the ground for four, and in McLean's next over there came a vintage Stewart on-drive, which took his score to 8 after facing 49 balls.

The following over from Walsh to Atherton was one of the finest you could ever hope to see. The first ball, a good length but just outside off, Atherton watched pass by. The second rapped him on the pads; there was a big appeal, but the ball was swinging so much that it was impossible for the umpire to say for certain that it would have hit the stumps, although it might well have done. The next was again fractionally outside off, and Atherton let it go. The fourth squared Atherton up completely, but just missed both bat and wicket. The next was almost identical, and so was the sixth. The relief on Atherton's face as he survived such an over was plain for all to see.

McLean then bowled a maiden to Stewart, and Walsh another one to Atherton, after which Walsh finished his spell, to be replaced by the spin of Nagamootoo. During the course of the morning's play Courtney Walsh had bowled eleven overs of which nine were maidens, but had taken only one wicket for four runs, and his figures were a true reflection of the quality of his bowling, not just a reflection of the fact that England were not particularly intent on scoring runs.

Nagamootoo now bowled a full toss to Atherton, which he dispatched to the square leg boundary with a flick of the wrist; a single off the next ball brought up his half-century, a typical Atherton innings, and crucial in the context of this match: if Atherton had gone early, the rest could follow quite quickly, as had often happened in the past.

With about ten minutes to go to lunch Jimmy Adams brought himself on to bowl at the pavilion end, and got a little turn out of the rough, but neither he nor Nagamootoo could break through the defence of the two English batsmen, and, after Stewart had hit Nagamootoo down the ground for four, Atherton followed suit, to bring up the England hundred. When lunch was taken at the end of that over, England's lead had progressed to 259, and things were not looking too good for the West Indies.

Lunch interval: England 130 - 3
Atherton n.o. 59 Stewart n.o. 20

The afternoon session began with a maiden from Nagamootoo to Stewart, who has always been much more comfortable with pace than with spin, then an over from McLean which yielded six runs, including a pull to mid-wicket by Atherton for four. Another miserly over from the spinner followed, then another sparkling boundary by Atherton off McLean, this time a cover drive. Then the pattern was repeated once more, with Atherton's boundary this time coming from a pull to fine leg. Up to this point the afternoon's six overs had yielded 18 runs, 3 off Nagamootoo, 15 off McLean, and the nearest the West Indies had come to taking a wicket was a half-hearted lbw appeal when the Atherton had edged the ball on to his pad, and two run-out attempts which were not really very close.

But that was soon to change. The first ball of Nagamootoo's next over was bowled very short, virtually a long hop, and Stewart played a cut shot. But the ball bounced unusually high, and Stewart only edged it to Campbell at second slip, who appeared to have been just as surprised as the batsman by the high bounce.

Stewart
c Campbell b Nagamootoo 25
Atherton n.o. 72 England 121 - 4

Vaughan came in to join Atherton, and now a quiet period ensued, with tidy bowling from Nagamootoo and Jimmy Adams, who had replaced McLean shortly after Stewart was out in order to give the fast bowlers a bit of a rest before taking the new ball, and by the time the afternoon drinks break came, only 15 runs had been added in the course of 12 overs.

After the drinks break Courtney Walsh returned to the attack, but not yet with the new ball; three singles came from his first over. To general surprise, however, the new ball was not taken at this point, and Nagamootoo was brought on at the Pavilion end. A maiden to Atherton then followed, with Nagamootoo getting more spin and more bounce than he had at the Vauxhall end.

Then Walsh struck again, with a slightly faster ball which nipped in off the seam, almost an off-break, and Vaughan was trapped plumb in front of his middle stump.

Vaughan lbw b Walsh 9
Atherton n.o. 80 England 139 - 5

Hick now replaced Vaughan, and played the first ball he received defensively, but the next, a leg-cutter this time, moved away from him, and he simply played the ball off the open face of the bat into the hands of Campbell at second slip, to become the second England player in the match to achieve a pair.

Hick c Campbell b Walsh 0
Atherton n.o. 80 England 139 - 6

England's lead was now 295, so the loss of two quick wickets at this stage was not as disastrous as it might have been, although they would prefer to add another 70 or 80 to their score. The West Indies had achieved enough to keep themselves interested; the new ball was there for the taking, and if they could get the remaining wickets cheaply they were still in with a chance. Admittedly it was only a slim chance, because only four West Indian sides in the past have ever scored over 300 to win a test, but the possibility could not yet be ruled out entirely, because the most recent of those occasions was against the Australians at Sydney as recently as 1999.

But Michael Atherton and Craig White were determined not to allow the England innings to collapse, and played sensibly, only attacking the occasional loose ball, although the fact that two such came in one over from Courtney Walsh, and Craig White was able to dispatch both of them for four, suggested that perhaps the West Indian fast bowler was feeling the effect of the lengthy spell he had bowled earlier in the day – this is one of the problems associated with continuing to play past the cricketer's normal retiring age!

Former England manager David Lloyd

There had been some speculation that the reason Ambrose was not bowling was because he had a calf strain, but now he took the ball and at once dropped onto his usual immaculate length, opening with a maiden. White then hit Walsh elegantly through the covers for four, whereupon the new ball was immediately taken. No further runs came from that over, but Atherton played a fine square drive for four off the first ball of Ambrose's next.

Then as Walsh started a new over White played a defensive push towards cover and set off for a single; Adrian Griffith ran in from point, picked up and threw under-arm to the bowler's end, and White was easily run out by the direct hit. Although the ball was played in front of the crease it appeared to have been Atherton who called for the run; White was on his back foot, and hesitated slightly, and this hesitation cost him his wicket.

**White run out (Griffith) 18
Atherton n.o. 86 England 163 - 7**

Atherton and Cork then played out the remaining two overs before tea, although Atherton had a slice of luck when he got an inside edge to a ball from Walsh and the ball narrowly missed his leg stump as it went down towards fine leg. By tea, England's lead had stretched to 325, and Atherton was still there.

**Tea interval: England 169 - 7
Atherton n.o. 89 Cork n.o. 1**

The West Indies' chances of winning now seemed to be receding, and they certainly could not afford to allow England to bat for very much longer, nor could they afford to allow them to score many more runs. England would be quite happy to use up another fifteen overs or so, because by that time their lead would probably be of the order of about 360, and they would not rate the West Indian chance of attaining that target very highly.

Ambrose resumed after tea for what would almost certainly be his final spell in test cricket; his first over would have been a maiden but for Cork edging the ball through the slips for four. After a maiden from Walsh Cork then hit a beautiful on-drive off Ambrose for another four, then two more boundaries came from Walsh's next

David Gower

over, one an elegant cover drive from Atherton just after surviving a very close lbw appeal, and the other an inside edge from Cork which went just past his stumps down to fine leg.

Ambrose was now limping, but bowled a maiden to Atherton none the less; then Cork hit Walsh, with a nonchalant flick of the wrist, over the fine leg boundary for six. A single put Atherton back on strike, and a fine shot off his legs to mid-wicket took his score to 99.

It was in Curtly Ambrose's next over that Atherton reached a well-deserved century, with a cut to third man for a single. This resolute and probably match-winning innings had taken 416 minutes and he had faced 315 balls; incredibly it was his first ever test century not only at the Oval but also in London, for he has never made one at Lord's either.

Atherton then faced another maiden from Walsh, who was astonished at having an lbw appeal turned down, although the ball had touched the bat first. For the next over Nixon McLean came on in place of Ambrose, and, after a short loosener which Cork pulled to mid-wicket for four and a rejected lbw appeal, he again hit Cork on the pads, and this time his appeal was granted.

Cork lbw b McLean 26
Atherton n.o. 100 England 207 - 8

Michael Vaughan bowling off-spin on the last morning

Caddick then came in, had one wild swing and played one defensive shot, and then wafted at a ball outside the off stump to be caught by the wicket-keeper.

Caddick c Jacobs b McLean 0
Atherton n.o. 100 England 207 - 9

Darren Gough was the last man in, and had a few lusty swings but without really connecting. Then after Atherton had pulled the first ball of a new over by Walsh to the mid-wicket boundary, the West Indian bowler eventually got his revenge by getting him to edge the last ball of his over to the wicket-keeper.

Atherton c Jacobs b Walsh 108
Gough n.o. 1 England 217 all out

So England had a lead of 373, and the West Indies needed 374 to win off a maximum of 104 overs, of which 14 remained to be bowled on this fourth day. Only twice in test history has such a target been reached, and no one now seriously considered a West Indian victory to be a possibility.

But the West Indies still had pride to play for, whilst England would fancy their chances of taking all ten wickets in the time available. They would hope to take one or two wickets before the close of play, but from a West Indian point of view, whether they were after a win or a draw, it was absolutely imperative that they end the day with all ten wickets still intact.

General mayhem as Thorpe collides with Sarwan

Sarwan receives medical attention after his collision with Graham Thorpe

The Fifth Day

The England bowlers did not in fact achieve the break-through they wanted, and the West Indian openers Campbell and Griffith played reasonably confidently against the bowling of Gough, who was replaced by White after five overs, and Caddick, who bowled unchanged till the close of play and who hit Griffith painfully on the chest immediately after he had been edged along the ground for four.

The West Indian pair took the score to 33 by the close, leaving 341 still to win, with 90 overs due to be bowled on the following day.

Close of play: West Indies 33 - 0 Campbell n.o. 15 Griffith n.o. 17

The weather forecast was good as the last day of the last test of the series dawned, and, unusually for the fifth day of a test match, not only was there a capacity crowd at the Oval, but 5,000 would-be spectators were locked out of the ground.

Some experts felt that it would prove easier to bat on this pitch today, although others were of the opinion that it would still give a lot of assistance to the bowlers – such feelings are typical of the grey areas which surround so many of the decisions made in test cricket; the proof of the pudding is in the eating!

England would feel that they would want to take two wickets before lunch, and three if Lara's was not one of the first two to fall. The West Indies would like to reach the lunch interval without losing a wicket, or at worst with only one wicket down, allowing Lara to try and take control of the run-chase.

Darren Gough opened the proceedings with a no-ball. His second was a full toss, which Campbell hit hard off a thick edge, wide of the slips for four. Two balls later the ball again found the boundary, this time from a square drive, so nine runs had come from the first three legitimate balls of the day. This was followed by a maiden over from Caddick, then six more runs came from Gough's second over, including another boundary to Campbell, this time a glance down to fine leg. Only two runs came from Caddick's next over, but they were enough to bring up the West Indies fifty, so 324 more runs were required, with 86 overs remaining.

Then Gough bowled to Campbell again. His first ball was an away-swinger outside the off stump, which Campbell allowed to pass by. His second ball was pitched well up, and flew off the edge of Campbell's bat into the normally safe hands of Graeme Hick at second slip, but for once this excellent slip catcher failed to hold the catch. Something even more unusual was about to happen. To a carbon copy of the previous delivery Campbell played the identical shot, and this time Hick made no mistake with the catch.

Campbell c Hick b Gough 28
Griffith n.o. 20 West Indies 50 - 1

This brought Brian Lara to the crease, earlier than in the first innings, perhaps indicating that the West Indies were still interested in chasing the target they had been set, because, if they

The crestfallen Sarwan leaves the field accompanied by the West Indian physiotherapist

were to stand any chance at all of reaching that target, Lara would have to be involved in the run-chase for as long a period as possible. The strategy would be for Griffith to play solidly at one end, allowing Lara to attack at the other.

But West Indian hopes were dealt a very severe blow in Caddick's next over, when he got a delivery to move away from Griffith, who edged the ball, and Stewart, diving both forward and to his left, made a spectacular catch.

**Griffith c Stewart b Caddick 20
Lara n.o. 0 West Indies 50 - 2**

Griffith's place was taken by another left-hander, Wavell Hinds. But if the West Indian batsmen were intending to launch an onslaught on the English bowlers, it did not come yet, and the next five overs only produced five runs. Then Gough got a ball to move away from Hinds, who edged yet another chance to Hick at second slip, and for the second time this morning Hick dropped the catch, and this time he did not get another chance off the next delivery. Hinds then celebrated by driving Gough through the covers for three runs.

But Wavell Hinds' good fortune was about to run out, for the very first ball of Andy Caddick's next over, an in-swinging yorker, hit Hinds on the toe and umpire Harper gave him out lbw.

**Hinds lbw b Caddick 7
Lara n.o. 1 West Indies 58 - 3**

The fall of this wicket did not necessarily mark the end of the road for the West Indies, but clearly, whether they were to win or draw this match, they could not afford to lose another wicket before lunch, because England would feel that once they had dismissed either Lara or Adams, they would be nearly home and dry.

If the West Indies were still hoping to win the match, they were certainly not going to take any risks at this stage, and they would need wickets in hand if they were to mount a one-day style attack late in the day.

The scoreboard as the end draws near

For the time being then, Lara and Adams played a normal, circumspect game, taking runs as and when they were available, but not taking any undue risks.

Gough and Caddick were then replaced by Cork and White, but this time the double bowling change did not have the dramatic results it had had in the first innings, although both bowlers were on the whole rather frugal: in fact only three boundaries were scored in between the fall of the third wicket and the lunch interval, but neither were there any undue alarms, and when lunch arrived Lara and Adams were still together, but the West Indies were still 285 runs short of their target.

Lunch interval: West Indies 89 - 3 Lara n.o. 17 Adams n.o. 14

After lunch the West Indies would need to start scoring faster if they were to maintain any chance of winning; if they did not score something in the region of a hundred runs between lunch and tea the target would be beyond even Adams and Lara, but they could not afford to take any chances. England needed to keep plugging away as they had been. The ball was still swinging, and inviting the batsmen to drive would be a good way of encouraging them to take risks.

The first over after lunch was bowled by Craig White, and after Adams took a single off the first ball, Lara then pulled the ball majestically to the mid-wicket boundary. If this caused West Indian supporters to harbour any thought of an exciting quest for runs

Curtly Ambrose putting bat to ball

being in the offing, the next over from Caddick would make them think again. After three defensive shots, Jimmy Adams flicked at a ball which pitched on leg stump, and White at backward square leg dived forward to take a very good catch.

Adams c White b Caddick 15
Lara n.o. 21 West Indies 94 - 4

Ramnaresh Sarwan survived the remaining two balls of Caddick's over, then Lara smashed White to the cover boundary with the most powerful shot of the day. Two overs later, he hit two further boundaries off Gough, and it was clear that he at least had not yet given up thoughts of a possible victory.

Neither, it seemed, had Sarwan, who in the next over hit Caddick through the covers for four and then to long-on for three. The runs continued to flow, with further boundaries by Sarwan, one off Cork and two off Caddick, and

at this stage 46 runs had been scored in the nine overs that had been bowled since the dismissal of Adams; Sarwan had already scored 27 off 31 balls.

But off the second ball of Cork's next over, Lara played a defensive push, and called his partner for a single. Sarwan responded, but Lara changed his mind and sent Sarwan back. Cork and Thorpe nearly collided as they both went for the ball, but Cork managed to pull out just in time. Thorpe seized the ball and, diving as he threw, broke the stumps at the bowler's end. Sadly for Sarwan, he collided with Thorpe, and was not only hurt in the collision, but was given out into the bargain, a very unfortunate end to a valuable and impressive innings.

Sarwan run out (Thorpe) 27
Lara n.o. 39 West Indies 140 - 5

In the next over Caddick produced a ball which swung away from Jacobs,

Courtney Walsh applauded on to the field by crowd, England players, and umpires alike

took the edge of his bat, and Hick took yet another catch at second slip.

Jacobs c Hick b Caddick 1
Lara n.o. 40 West Indies 142 - 6

All thoughts of a West Indian victory had now finally disappeared, and the big question was whether they would be able to play out the remaining time and claim a draw. With about 50 overs left and six wickets down, this was looking increasingly unlikely.

Caddick's first ball to Nagamootoo produced a leg-bye, and then Lara showed that he was not deterred by pulling the next delivery over mid-wicket for four; he then took a single from the last ball of the over to keep the strike.

But then, after Lara flicked Gough down to fine leg for two, he was hit on the pad and, in response to Gough's appeal, umpire Shepherd gave him out. It is rare for David Shepherd to make an umpiring mistake, but on this occasion the television replays showed that in fact the ball had pitched fractionally outside Lara's leg stump, and although there is no doubt that it would have gone on to hit the wicket, it should have been given not out. But umpires do not have the benefit of television replays for leg before decisions, and with a ball being bowled at nearly 90 mph it is hardly surprising that mistakes are sometimes made. Be that as it may, Lara was now out, and only the West Indian tail stood between England and the victory they wanted so badly.

Lara lbw b Gough 47
Nagamootoo n.o. 0
West Indies 150 - 7

McLean now came to join Nagamootoo, and they added 17 in the next four overs, including some very good forceful shots from Nagamootoo. Then Gough produced yet another full length away-swinger, found the edge of Nagamootoo's bat,

The final blow: Courtney Walsh falls lbw to Cork to give England victory

and Hick once more failed to hold the catch – although on this occasion he was somewhat impeded by Graham Thorpe who also dived to take it – and the ball carried on to reach the boundary. Four balls later though, Nagamootoo was hit on the pad, umpire Shepherd raised his finger, and this time there was no mistake.

Nagamootoo lbw b Gough 13
McLean n.o. 4 West Indies 167 - 8

Then followed one of the most extraordinary scenes ever witnessed on a test ground. When Curtly Ambrose came out to bat for his last innings in test cricket, not only did he receive a standing ovation from the entire crowd, but also the England team – and the umpires – lined up to form a guard of honour and applauded him all the way to the wicket. But if it put older spectators in mind of Bradman's last innings on the same ground in 1948, Ambrose did not suffer the same indignity as the great Australian, who was out first ball in his final innings; he stoutly defended the yorker with which Darren Gough greeted him.

In fact the farewell party was to last a little longer yet for Ambrose, for he was still at the crease when the tea interval came eight overs later, and had three fours to his name; he had also helped his side to pass 200. What was more, he had two more standing ovations, one as he left the field before tea and another when he re-emerged from the pavilion to begin the final session.

Tea interval: West Indies 205 - 8
McLean n.o. 17 Ambrose n.o. 24

The outcome of the match, of course, was no longer in doubt; there was no serious possibility of McLean, Ambrose and Walsh lasting out for the 37 overs which still remained to be bowled. But no one left the ground, and the cricket was just as intense as it had been throughout the match.

Cork and Gough grab the stumps and run at the end of the match

Two overs and four balls later, Ambrose flashed at a ball from Cork, and gave a straightforward catch to Michael Atherton at first slip. As he slowly and soulfully left the field, he received yet another standing ovation – how many cricketers ever get four standing ovations in one innings?

A few seconds later the crowd was on its feet again to greet Courtney Walsh. Unlike Ambrose, Walsh had not said that he would definitely retire at the end of this series, but it was clear to all that this would be his last test in England, and so he was accorded the same welcome as Ambrose, including the guard of honour of the England players.

But Walsh was not to last as long as Ambrose, and the second ball he received from Cork hit him on the pad; the umpire's finger went up, and the match was over.

Walsh lbw b Cork 0
McLean n.o. 23
West Indies 215 all out

England won by 158 runs

So England won the series 3 - 1, the first time they had won a series against the West Indies since 1969, and the first time they had won a five-match series against them since 1957. It had been a truly memorable series, played in a sportsmanlike spirit all too rarely seen these days; a series which was enjoyed by all who witnessed it, both those who appreciated the subtleties behind the visible events and those who simply like to see runs scored and wickets tumble, but, as in all first-class cricketing contests, England's was a psychological victory as much as a physical one.

Dermot Reeve (left) and David Gower prepare for the presentation ceremony

Men of the Series: Courtney Walsh and Darren Gough

Nasser Hussain holding the Wisden Trophy

Match Scorecard

England	First Innings		Second Innings	
Atherton	b Mclean	83	c Jacobs b Walsh	108
Trescothick	c Campbell b Nagamootoo	78	c Lara b Ambrose	7
Hussain	c Jacobs b Nagamootoo	0	lbw b McLean	0
Thorpe	lbw b Walsh	40	c Griffith b Walsh	10
Stewart	lbw b Mclean	0	c Griffith b Nagamootoo	25
Vaughan	lbw b Ambrose	10	lbw b Walsh	9
Hick	lbw b Ambrose	17	c Campbell b Walsh	0
White	not out	11	run out (Griffith)	18
Cork	lbw b Mclean	0	lbw b McLean	26
Caddick	c Hinds b Walsh	4	c Jacobs b McLean	0
Gough	b Walsh	8	not out	1
Extras	b 4, lb 15, w 1, nb 10	30	b 1, lb 7, nb 5	13
Total	(123.4 overs, 509 min)	281	(108 overs, 444 min)	217

Fall of wickets:
First innings: 1-159, 2-159, 3-184, 4-184, 5-214, 6-254, 7-254, 8-255, 9-264
Second innings: 1-21, 2-29, 3-56, 4-121, 5-139, 6-139, 7-163, 8-207, 9-207
Bowling
Ambrose 31-8-38-2, Walsh 35.4-16-68-3   Ambrose 22-8-36-1, Walsh38-17-73-4
McLean 29-6-80-3, Nagamootoo 24-7-63-2   McLean 22-5-60-3, Nagamootoo19-7-29-1
Adams 4 - 0 -13 - 0   Adams 7 - 3- 11- 0

West Indies	First Innings			
Campbell	b Cork	20	c Hick b Gough	28
Griffith	c Hick b White	6	c Stewart b Caddick	20
Hinds	lbw b Cork	2	lbw b Caddick.	7
Lara	b White	0	lbw b Gough	47
Adams	c Hick b Cork	5	c White b Caddick	15
Sarwan	c Trescothick b White	5	run out (Thorpe)	27
Jacobs	not out	26	c Hick b Caddick	1
Nagamootoo	c Trescothick b Gough	18	lbw b Gough	13
Ambrose	lbw b Caddick	0	c Atherton b Cork	28
McLean	b White	29	not out	23
Walsh	b Whitet	5	lbw b Cork	0
Extras	lb 3, nb 6	6	lb 3, w 1, nb 2	6
Total	(50.5 overs, 233 min)	125	(70 overs, 210 min)	215

Fall of wickets:
1-32, 2-32, 3-32, 4-34, 5-39, 6-51, 7-74, 8-75, 9-119
1-50, 2-50, 3-58, 4-94, 5-140, 6-142, 7-150, 8-167, 9-215
Bowling:
Gough 13-3-25-1, Caddick 18-7-42-1   Gough 20-3-64-3, Caddick 21-7-54-4
White 11.5-1-32-5, Cork 8-3-23-3   White 11-2-32-0, Cork 15-1-50-2
          Vaughan 3-1-12-0

England won by 158 runs